Getting A Life

Getting A Life

How to Find Your True Vocation

Renée M. LaReau

ORBIS BOOKS

Maryknoll, New York 10545

Founded in 1970, Orbis Books endeavors to publish works that enlighten the mind, nourish the spirit, and challenge the conscience. The publishing arm of the Maryknoll Fathers and Brothers, Orbis seeks to explore the global dimensions of the Christian faith and mission, to invite dialogue with diverse cultures and religious traditions, and to serve the cause of reconciliation and peace. The books published reflect the views of their authors and do not represent the official position of the Maryknoll Society. To learn more about Maryknoll and Orbis Books, please visit our website at www.maryknoll.org.

Library of Congress Cataloging-in-Publication Data

LaReau, Renée M.
    Getting a life : how to find your true vocation / by Renée M. LaReau.
      p. cm.
    ISBN 1-57075-498-5 (pbk.)
    1. Vocation – Christianity.   I. Title.
  BV4740 .L37 2003
  248.8'4 – dc21

                                             2003009206

In memory of Gretchen Anne LaReau

My sister "Gretchy"

1979–1993

In such a short time, she lived quite a life.

I know that she is guiding me as I continue to live mine.

Contents

Acknowledgments   9

Introduction   11

1. Becoming You   17

2. Discernment: Asking the Big Questions   37

3. Stop Signs: Rejections, Failures, Mistakes, and Limits   54

4. Living in the Sun and the Shade   70

5. Living to Work, Working to Live   89

6. Community Matters   105

7. Mentors and Models   123

8. Road Rules   140

Epilogue: A Glance Forward   157

Acknowledgments

I am very grateful to the many people who offered their insights to be shared in this book and to those whose stories appear in its pages: Justin LaReau, Jim Schmiedeler, Mike Schmiedeler, Cheryl Healy, Emily Portune, Laura Portune, Emily Trick, Sylvia and John Dillon, and the "Winchell Neighborhood Crew" in Kalamazoo. Their lives continue to be inspirations to me, and I am thankful for their friendship.

I would also like to thank the people who took the time to read and comment on my manuscript, both in parts and in its entirety: Anne Trick, Jennifer and Matthew Tilghman-Havens, Rev. John Cusick, and Kathleen Rossman, O.S.F. Peggy Braner, with her meticulous attention to detail, helped me to root out most of the typos in the early stages.

I offer a special word of thanks to the people of St. Charles Borromeo Parish, who continually encouraged me in my writing and provided me with daily examples of generosity. I am particularly grateful to editor and publisher Michael Leach for taking a chance and giving a wonderful opportunity to a first-time author.

My parents, Al and Rita LaReau, continue to support and guide me as they always have since day one, and never without the usual doses of humor and wisdom.

Introduction

I always imagined when I was a kid that adults had some kind of inner toolbox, full of shiny tools: the saw of discernment, the hammer of wisdom, the sandpaper of patience. But then when I grew up I found that life handed you these rusty bent old tools — friendships, prayer, conscience, honesty — and said, Do the best you can with these, they will have to do. And mostly, against all odds, they're enough.
                                                    —Anne Lamott, *Traveling Mercies*

I remember the conversation so well, though a few years have passed now. My friend and I are on the phone again in the middle of the day. She is working as an administrator at the same university where I am in graduate school. We chat about our friends, discuss the upcoming weekend, and plan when we can next meet for lunch. Inevitably our conversation shifts to where it always does: "Renée, what am I going to *do* with my life?" she howls into the phone with great gusto. My friend seems to have it all: a senior-level administrative position at a prestigious university, a master's degree, a fun and loving group of friends. I can't imagine why she would be dissatisfied with her life. She is one of those people I think of as "having it all together."

Yet for all that she has going for her, she still struggles with the fact that she misses teaching, a profession she left three years ago. She is growing disillusioned with her current job and wonders if there might be a better way for her to use her many talents. In addition, she lives two thousand miles away from her family and the distance is starting to wear on her. Her question perturbs me, as it always does, because I'm wondering the same thing. What am I supposed to *do* with my life?

"I don't know," I say to her softly, bewilderedly, thinking, "Why is she asking *me?*" I am exhausted. I am nearing the end of my graduate program and am in the midst of my job search. I can think of five completely different kinds of jobs I would like to have in the near future. Each seems to pull and tug at me with equal force. In addition, I am dating someone who lives almost three hundred miles away and fear that I will not find a job in the city where he lives. I do not yet know if he is "the one" and am frustrated by my indecision. Questions about career and relationships overwhelm me, and I wonder where my faith fits in with it all. Though my situation differs from hers, I share her frustrations and questions.

"When are we going to have all of this figured out?" my friend and I ask each other, and the conversation seems to go in circles. We try to help each other out, offering advice and analysis as we always do. After hanging up the phone, I feel better having voiced my frustrations, and I sense that she does too. I quietly, inwardly give thanks for her friendship. I am thankful to have someone like her with whom to share and reflect on some of these big questions, questions about career, education, priorities, relationships, family, and gifts and talents.

That particular conversation is very typical of those I've had with various friends and acquaintances throughout our twenties. Our thoughtful phone, e-mail, and in-person discussions persist as we continue to ponder possible career choices, grapple with dating and the possibility of marriage, navigate now-adult relationships with family, friends, and colleagues, and formulate opinions and responses to the day's news headlines.

Our twenties are great, in a sense. We have the whole world ahead of us and have a multitude of choices at our fingertips. We're young and energetic, full of ideas and potential. Yet we grapple with a fairly high level of tumult and stress as we find our initial footing in careers and relationships. Dating can be difficult. The work force can be draining and disillusioning. Locating a faith community that is both comforting and challenging can seem nearly impossible. Friendships and family relationships often shift unpredictably under our feet as we navigate major life changes.

There is a very good reason that the publisher of the book *The Quarterlife Crisis,* written by two twenty-five-year-old authors, has sold so many copies to people in their twenties. There is some sort of unwritten rule in our culture that reminds us repeatedly that we'd better have it all together by the time we are thirty. With this unwritten rule of "get it together before you're thirty" dutifully internalized, we feel that we live in a kind of pressure cooker as we try to figure out who it is we are supposed to become, what we are to accomplish, who the key people in our lives are meant to be, and how our faith should inform our life choices.

My dad, who is in his fifties, shared with me a conversation he had recently with his running buddies. As they cruised through the early morning darkness together, they talked about which age they would revisit if they could. The three Baby Boomers all decided that thirty-five would be the perfect age to return to. Twenty-five? No way, they all agreed. Despite the youth and vigor that characterize that age, none of them had the slightest desire to return to their twenties. I can see why.

We have even more choices than the generations that have preceded us, and this multitude of options gives rise to a complicated decision-making process. I remember having a difficult conversation with my dad one evening as I was trying to choose a graduate school. He said to me, "When I was your age, you just graduated from college, went on to professional school, and got a job. There was none of this 'finding yourself' stuff. You pursued law, medicine, or business, and made a career of one of those three professions."

Our generation, on the other hand, is more likely to change jobs six or seven times within a lifetime. We are waiting longer to marry, find a meaningful career, or embark on a journey to the religious life. We are taking more time to wrestle with those big questions that require a lot of discernment and energy: Where will I live? Which of my childhood or college friendships will I continue to maintain? Should I attend graduate school or enter the work force? Should I marry this person I'm dating? What kind of career should I pursue? How will my faith fit into all of this? What is my response to be to the needs I see in the world? Though these questions all involve discrete issues, there is a deeper, underlying question that undergirds all of them: What is God calling to me to do with my life? Phrased another way, it could be: What is my vocation? This question of vocation is the fundamental question that undergirds and suffuses all of the others and is the question I've chosen as the focus of this book. How *do* we find our true vocation? And once we do find it, how do we really *live* it?

My sense, thus far, is that it takes a lifetime of ongoing discernment to hear God's call and build our lives around it. It takes a lifetime for us to discern what our part will be in building up the Kingdom of God. It takes a lifetime to fully discover and find the strength to live out our vocation. I do not pretend to have all the answers, but there are a few things I've learned along the way as I've tried to build the foundation for my own life. Friends, mentors, family, and colleagues have given me a few tools for decision-making that have helped me tremendously. There are some tools that I've been given that I don't yet know how to use. I've acquired some tools by observing people I admire, and some have come to me through persistent prayer. Some have hit me over the head when I've been too busy or ignorant to pick them up myself.

Though we supply the "human power" to build our lives, we are guided by the best possible architect. As we try to piece together the different components of our lives, God stands over our shoulders, lovingly crafted design in hand, guiding and encouraging us to build the life that we are called to build. Though we are free to make our own decisions, God holds the vision before us of what we can be, what our world can be. God oversees the life journeys of individuals, neighborhoods, cities, and nations, and guides us all.

The process of discerning a particular vocation takes a long time, as the late Archbishop Oscar Romero reminds us in his famous prayer: "We lay foundations that will need further development.... We are workers, not master builders, ministers, not messiahs." All of us, the workers, are in this together. We build lives not to live in comfortable solitude, but to live within the challenging and supporting bounds of community. We want to build a life that both fulfills us personally and meets a need in wider society. We want to find a vocation that both utilizes our talents and meets a need in the world.

It is a relief to know that God, the ultimate builder, the "chief architect," is in charge of this process of building a life, of discovering our vocation, but we still have our work cut out for us. We have many important decisions to make, and our twenties are rife with opportunity and replete with potential as we plan our lives and let our lives happen to us. Building a life is a combination of putting in a hard day's work and stepping back to take in the long view, the big picture. A variety of tools is required as we build up and pare down, mold and measure our lives. I hope you find some of these tools helpful as you listen for God's call, begin to build your own life, and discover and nurture your own vocation. See you around the neighborhood.

❧ *One* ❧

Becoming You

May you be blessed with passion,
and may you follow it all your life.
— Sr. Helen Prejean

I dwell in possibility.
— Emily Dickinson

I never used to think the word "vocation" applied to me, or to any of my friends for that matter. In my mind, vocation was what my high school teachers talked about when they tried to recruit the boys in my class to become priests. Vocation was for those holy people, not for the cast of characters I hung out with and spent time with. Vocation was only for people who lived apart from the world, not in the midst of it. It was a pious concept that I never felt I could relate to. I heard people speak of "having a vocation" or "being called by God," and I thought to myself, "Well, isn't that nice...but that isn't for people like me." The whole concept of vocation was pretty much an irrelevant mystery.

But something happened to me gradually in my twenties as I went through college and graduate school, developed friendships, and entered the working world. I began to sense that this concept of "vocation" wasn't nearly as narrow as I'd thought. I began to develop a limited understanding of the concept. I began to catch some "glimpses of grace," hints that God was at work in the lives of my friends and family, that each of us was being called by God in our own way. These "glimpses of grace" took many forms: the looks on some friends' faces on the day of their weddings, the excitement and energy in my classmate's voice when she was offered a fantastic job, a great dinnertime conversation with old friends, an outpouring of compassion at a young person's funeral. I began to sense that there was a greater purpose, a bigger picture encapsulating all of these graced moments that took place in the context of my little life. I recalled reading the words of spiritual writer Henri Nouwen: "My deepest vocation is to be a witness to the glimpses of God I have been allowed to catch." I began to sense that I had caught the glimpses and that some response was required from me. I just wasn't sure where to go from there. I wasn't sure what my response was supposed to be.

Through the grace-filled moments that I experienced, I began to sense that a God I'd once thought was distant and mysterious was actually quite close and communicative. I began to think that maybe the concept of vocation *did* have something to do with my own life and the lives of those around me. I began to sense God *did* try to communicate with me, somehow, in almost imperceptible ways.

I realize now that certain reactions and feelings I'd had at particular times in my life had something to do with whether or not I was listening for God's call, whether I was becoming "me," the person God was calling me to be. I remember at some points just going about my daily business and really feeling in my gut like I was doing the right thing. All the important details were falling into place, and I was making good choices. And there were some times when I felt that the way I was living my life was all wrong, dead wrong, completely wrong. I'm just beginning to realize now that those gut feelings and critical sensibilities were somehow tied in with my burgeoning sense of vocation and were connected to whether or not I was living the sort of life God was calling me to live.

Thanks to some good books, a few fine mentors, and the passage of time, I developed a fledgling awareness that *I* could have a vocation, and so could my friends and other people I knew. I never had a particular "God experience" or "a mountaintop experience" like some people talk about — no visions, no voices whispering in my ear. My increased awareness of vocation has been more of a gradual sharpening of consciousness that God is active in the lives of people I know and is at work in my own life as well. I slowly have become aware that life, in all of its struggles and triumphs, is tinged with grace, suffused with the holy. Though I don't know that I could define what grace is, I have begun to grasp what the German theologian Karl Rahner said, unbelievably, in the last painful minutes before he died: *All is grace!* I have begun to grasp what the lyrics of the U2 song "Grace" might be about when they say, "Grace finds goodness in everything / Grace finds beauty in everything." Life is grace. Living out a vocation is our acceptance of and witness to God's gift of grace.

"Grace" and "holy" are words I have been hesitant to use when I talk about my own life or that of my friends. We make mistakes. We can be pretty irreverent most of the time. We do crazy things. "Grace" and "holiness" are such strong words. But I am getting more and more comfortable with them, especially as I watch the people in my life develop into some pretty incredible individuals. They are not superheroes, but good, solid, well-intentioned people who I know are going to make a difference in the world. Grace and holiness don't preclude mistakes, horrible days, bad moods, quick tempers. Grace and holiness encompass these things, and that is what makes us truly human. We are graced and holy because of and in spite of our shortcomings. To recognize our vocation is first to acknowledge that our lives are graced and holy.

The monk and spiritual writer Thomas Merton, in an oft-quoted passage from his book *Conjectures of a Guilty Bystander,* describes how he felt when he suddenly grasped the goodness and the giftedness of people around him as he stood on a busy street corner in Louisville, Kentucky. The famous passage reads:

> In Louisville, on the corner of 4th and Walnut, in the center of the shopping district, I was suddenly overwhelmed with the realization that I loved all these people, that they were mine and I was theirs. There is no way of telling people that they are all walking around shining like the sun.

I doubt that, as he stood on the corner of 4th and Walnut, Merton had a vision of businesspeople sporting halos or families

sprouting angel wings. What he did observe was a basic goodness in people, a core of holiness that remained solid despite their
shortcomings. He saw that they shone like the sun. He saw that humanity was graced and holy. Since I've read that Merton passage
I've attempted to see humankind as he saw it on that ordinary day
when he had such an extraordinary revelation. Though I would
never claim that my own observations have reached the level
of mystical insight, I have benefited from Merton's street corner
epiphany. I've grown to love watching the crowds in airports for
this reason.

I remember one occasion in particular when I was traveling to
Iowa and my flight was delayed. I was stuck at Chicago's O'Hare
International Airport for three hours. Instead of reading by my departure gate I parked myself in the food court in the center of the
terminal. The scene was fascinating. I watched people as they
dunked their donuts and polished off enormous burritos. I observed parents trying to keep their little children occupied with
French fries and businesspeople talking on their cell phones and
reading the *New York Times.* I told more than three people what
time it was and made small talk with a man from India. I saw
people who approached travel with an air of sophistication and
people who looked like they were flying for the very first time. The
whole scene was a beautiful, buzzing picture of humanity. To put
it simply, I just had a deep sense that the people I was watching
were good people — people on a journey trying to get where they
needed to go. Even in a chaotic airport terminal, grace stood out
in sharp relief against a whirlwind backdrop of activity.

Recognizing that we have a vocation means recognizing our
core level of holiness, our basic goodness that comes from being
made in God's image. We shine like the sun, as Merton phrased it.
This core of holiness that we have remains solid despite all that
we sometimes do to try to erode it. And *that* is grace. Our holiness
is pure gift. God's grace is unconditional and is doled out in great
quantities. It cannot be given or taken away by anyone or anything.
It is ours to keep and acknowledge as we wish. Grace and holiness
are pure gifts that invite a response from us, a response that both
fulfills us personally and meets a need in the world.

What Is Vocation Anyway?

The concept of vocation comes from the Latin word *vocare,* meaning "to call." The call, of course, comes from God, and our role is to hear and respond to that call. It sounds so simple. Then why is it so hard? Why can the process of finding our niche in the world become so laborious? Why can the concept of vocation sometimes seem elusive?

Part of the difficulty is that the way we discover a vocation is very different from how we go about most of our everyday business. Our whole lives are geared toward pursuing goals, and there are certain ways one goes about that: take the right courses in college, acquire the right internships and work experience, save some money, put yourself in contact with the bigwigs and giants in your profession. It seems that most of life is about working hard, pursuing goals, and having ambitions. To get *this* job you have to go to *this* school and live in *this* city and schmooze with *these* people.

But vocation is different. It requires a different type of discipline than our usual ambitions require. Vocation asks us to try on a different mindset. Vocation, as defined by educator and spiritual writer Parker Palmer, "does not mean a goal that I pursue. It means a calling that I hear." Vocation is not so much something we work toward as it is something we listen for. Vocation means increased consciousness. It means learning to listen for the voice of God and becoming the person you are called to be. Vocation means learning to pay attention.

Learning to pay attention is really difficult, because life is busy, noisy, and messy. Life as young professionals and students is extremely hectic. Long hours at work and school, competing obligations, or the absence of a good support system can make it very difficult to hear the voice of God. I remember one day in particular, about a year ago, when life's continuous craziness and busyness completely caught up with me.

It was a Sunday afternoon, and I had a few hours of free time before it would be time to iron some clothes, pack a lunch, and get ready for the start of the workweek. I sat on the couch reading the newspaper, and I looked up and suddenly realized that my entire house was a complete, disgusting mess. That quiet Sunday afternoon was the first time in weeks that I had actually slowed down enough just to look around me. The condition of the house I was living in was just one of many indications that my chosen pace of life was spinning out of control. I had been at work nonstop for the past few weeks and had neglected other aspects of my life. I wrote in my journal that day:

> Somehow the month of May has escaped me. I'm sitting here in the whirlwind that is my house. My two roommates have moved out but all their stuff is for some reason still here. There are boxes everywhere and I just now washed the pots and dishes I used three days ago to make macaroni and cheese. I have just opened my Visa card statement and found that it has an unauthorized charge of $2900 on it. I have no idea how it got there. I'm looking at some Easter egg decorations on my coffee table, and realizing that Easter was two months ago. For dinner I just ate two frozen Reese's Peanut Butter Cups, a hot pretzel, and some microwave popcorn. I can't remember when I last went grocery shopping.

To this day I'm not exactly sure why I described that scene in such detail in my journal. I may have done so because I felt that my physical surroundings were a sign of how I'd let other priorities in my life slip because of work. I hadn't caught up with friends or family much and hadn't made enough time for exercise. Those few quiet hours spent with the Sunday paper allowed me to realize that I needed to slow down, get my house in order, and make time for the important things I'd neglected. Busyness and chaos are among the biggest obstacles to the practices of listening and paying attention, and it is important to acknowledge the formidable challenges they present. It is hard to reflect on your life's calling when you can't even make sense of your own living space!

Life is busy and hectic, and it may seem as if we have no time (or make no time) to reflect on the direction that our life is headed. Yet life is a continuous opportunity to listen to, share, and respond to the ways in which God calls us — in our careers, in our relationships, in our roles in the church, in our communities and in our world. Exploring our vocation gives us an opportunity to develop our awareness and understanding *of a reality that is already taking place* — the life of Christian discipleship that God calls all of us to live. That is one of the best parts about vocation: It is a reality that is already taking place and already going on.

We don't have to create a vocation for ourselves — it is already there. The pursuit of vocation is not a matter of inventing something new for ourselves; it is a matter of paying more attention to a reality that is always taking place. The pursuit of a vocation means listening for a gift that we have already been offered by a generous God. In the midst of busyness and chaos, God invites us to carve out some room in our lives to reflect and listen.

Since I've started to think about this concept of "learning to listen," I've noticed a certain knee-jerk reaction I have when I'm sitting in church. This reaction is usually stirred up after the homily, when somebody reads the petitions and then it comes time for people to voice their own prayer intentions. Inevitably someone prays for an increase in vocations. This particular petition does not sit very well with me anymore. What I wish people would pray for (and maybe at some point I'll have the guts to voice this myself) is for an *increased awareness* of *all* of our vocations.

There is no need to pray for an increase in vocations. The vocations already exist. We all have one, even those of us who consider ourselves "piety-impaired" and have trouble thinking of ourselves as called by God. There is no vocation crisis in our churches, at least in the way it is traditionally understood. The real crisis is that sometimes we do not realize that the way we are living our lives is within the context of a call from God.

Looking for Patterns

Vocation calls us to a sharpened consciousness, a new awareness of the events and people around us. Learning the practices of listening and paying attention sometimes means taking a look at our pasts and looking for patterns. In the discernment of a vocation, a look at our past decisions can help us choose a good direction for our future.

In some ways, this practice is similar to the practice of mowing the lawn. I use mowing the lawn as an analogy because it is something I love to do, although I don't get to do it too often anymore. When I mow the lawn I get to be outside and blow off some steam. The freshly cut grass smells wonderful, and the results of my work are apparent immediately. Mowing the lawn is a very satisfying kind of labor in that it provides instant gratification. Results are immediate. An added bonus is that a freshly cut lawn even makes the neighbors happy. The neighborhood street looks neater when everyone takes care of their yard.

While I mow the lawn I tend to look only at what is right in front of me. I try to avoid rocks and sticks. I try to push a straight path with the mower and create neat, consecutive rows. I observe the contrast between the neatness of the mowed sections of grass and the scraggly, unkempt nature of the unfinished sections. It's not usually until I'm about halfway done that I can look across the yard and see the kind of pattern I've established in the grass. It is very gratifying to see the neat rows that I've mowed one at a time. I also see a few narrow, tall tufts of grass — the spots I've missed. I observe that many of the rows are consistent and straight, but there are some that are a bit crooked.

I have to mow the lawn for a while before I can see these patterns emerge. When I've finished mowing about half the yard I can see what kind of lawn-mower I am and make the necessary adjustments to finish the rest of the yard. Living out a vocation happens in a similar way. You live for a while, dealing with what is right in front of you. You push and press on, trying to avoid pitfalls. After a while, you look back on your decisions, look back on your tendencies and patterns of behavior. You evaluate what you have done well and what needs more work, and you make the necessary adjustments for the future.

This *modus operandi* has worked pretty well for me as I make decisions about the future of my career. I try to look to the past to determine which direction I should turn in the future. Sometimes I look back at my past decisions and think, "Okay I'm never doing *that* again," and sometimes I say to myself, "Wow, I'm so glad I chose to do things *this* way." Listening for the voice of vocation is about intentionally letting our past inform our future. It is good to step back, occasionally, to look at the results of our work, our decisions. It is important to look back and see what kind of "lawn mowers" we have been.

Paying attention to our past patterns can help us a great deal in determining the authenticity of our vocation. For example, during the past few years I've discovered, gradually, that I have a vocation as a writer. When I look back on my life now I can see certain indications that I was meant to be a writer, but if you had asked me earlier in life I wouldn't have been so sure. I had always thought that I would have a science-related career. Teachers and mentors had always told me that I was gifted in the sciences. I liked biology and chemistry experiments, and even attended a math- and science-oriented high school. My parents were both in the medical field, so I was comfortable and familiar with those career choices and the lifestyle those occupations enabled. Science and medicine were what I knew, and they were all I knew. A career in any other area was unthinkable.

As far as writing was concerned, I knew that I enjoyed it, but I saw it merely as a hobby. I didn't really know any writers personally and didn't see writing as a viable career option. So I started college as a biology major and took all the right courses and necessary steps to go to medical school. I worked dutifully to complete my organic chemistry labs, memorized the biological cycles, and attended all the pre-medicine informational meetings, but it never seemed like a very good fit. I could not get excited about making plans to attend medical school. I dragged my feet when the time arrived to study for the MCAT. I struggled in upper-level science classes and didn't really enjoy what I was doing. I don't know that I was all that good at it either.

On the other hand, I loved my elective courses that allowed me to write papers and discuss literature with my peers. I kept a journal throughout college that was a soothing outlet when life became chaotic or confusing. Friends would tell me how much they loved receiving my letters during our summer correspondence. Even with all these factors, I never considered writing as something I could pursue as a career. It took me a while before I was far enough from my childhood, teenage, and even college years to see certain emerging patterns that indicated that writing would be a good choice for me, and an extraordinarily meaningful life pursuit.

I look back now and see the cumulative pile of evidence that indicated that writing would play a significant role in my future. The indications comprise images and memories: childhood memories of trips home from the library with stacks of books that piled up to eye level when I carried them. Careful, conscientious participation in school spelling bees. Indignant notes written to my parents on construction paper and slipped under their bedroom door. A cache of letters I'd written to famous people, like the general managers of the Chicago White Sox and Chicago Cubs. I had never set out to become a writer. As I look back at this spate of evidence now, however, it makes sense to me that I am slowly becoming one. Becoming a writer feels right—*so* right, in a way that taking biology courses and applying to medical school definitely did not.

That doesn't mean that there aren't days now when I despise writing. Nothing kills a writer's spirit like a looming deadline or a complete lack of inspiration. Whenever I have a specific project deadline in front of me, I can think of a thousand other topics I'd rather write about. I sit at my laptop computer and convince myself that my career is doomed, that what I once thought was a gift for writing is really a giant farce, and tomorrow, when I e-mail this article to my editor, I am going to be discovered as a mere one-hit wonder, like some of the bands I listened to on the Top 40 radio stations in the 1980s. Despite the fact that I usually meet my deadlines, I still often stress and work myself up into a frenzy each time a new one rolls around.

Some of my mentors, thankfully, have assured me that these fears and trepidations are completely normal. One of them often reminds me of a quote from Robert Louis Stevenson: "I hate to write, but I *love* to have written." I find comfort in this, knowing that in my fears and frustrations, I am in good company. It's good to know that even the author of *Treasure Island* and *Kidnapped* fought his battles with the self-doubt that often accompanies the writing process.

Though I would define my writing work as a vocation, that insight hasn't eliminated the challenges and struggles I still have with the profession. Now that I have had some time to look back at patterns in my life, I can recognize that these struggles and frustrations are part of a bigger picture. They're like the rocks, twigs, and sticks that are inevitably going to get caught up in the lawn mower from time to time: they are an annoyance, but after we kick them up with the mower we can get on with the rest of the yard, and as a result, we are more aware of their presence in the future. Finding a vocation doesn't preclude frustration, discouragement, or worry. When you find your true vocation, however, you somehow don't let those things get in your way. When you find your true vocation, you are willing to work through them with a greater purpose in mind.

God Doesn't Give Up

In discerning a vocation it is helpful to look back and identify past patterns. It also helps to remember that it is God who initiates and God who calls. God is the source of vocation and, thankfully, God is very, very persistent. Not identifying your vocation right away is not like missing a flight. God is not a pilot who takes off without us. God keeps waiting and continues to announce our flight number, hoping we will listen because there are extensive travels in store for us.

God continually encourages each of us: "Become you. Become the person I am calling you to be." Theologians have debated for years whether or not God has a specific plan in mind for each of us and have argued over where our free will fits in with this plan. I am no theologian, but my sense thus far is that though God has no blueprint for us, God always invites us forward, encourages us toward growth, and promises to be persistently present during the process. God always calls us to be more, to be fuller, to be deeper. Having a vocation means that God continually invites us forward throughout our lives. Having a vocation means that God does not give up on us.

Discovering God's persistence has been a relief for me, since there have been more times than I can count that I haven't listened to God. I've thought that, surely, I can figure my life out on my own, if I just have enough ambition and drive. All too often I save communication with God for those times when I am in deep jams. Most of the time, however, I feel pretty self-sufficient. "I can handle it," I confidently convince myself.

My Type A personality regularly threatens to take over as the guiding force in my life. I have readily identified with the novelist Anna Quindlen's description of her own ambition: "At twenty-five I should have worn a big red A on my chest; it would have stood for ambition, an ambition so brazen and burning that it would have reduced Hester Prynne's transgression to pale pink." I still continually fight the feeling that whatever I am going to accomplish is going to result from my efforts alone. It is hard for me to remember that it is not entirely up to me to find my place in the world and do what I was meant to do.

Graduate school courses in theology have provided me with a more sophisticated diagnosis of my tendencies. I realize now that my unrelenting independence and desire for achievement are actually quite reminiscent of some of the heretics in the early Christian church. These well-intentioned folks were called the Pelagians, and they were deemed heretics because they believed that salvation was a do-it-yourself kind of thing. In other words, if the Pelagians were around today, Home Depot would be their favorite store. Who needs an electrician or a carpenter when you can purchase the home improvement kit yourself? Who needs God when you've got the smarts and the wherewithal to map out your own life's course? The Pelagians tended to rely too much on their own efforts and push God outside the picture a little too often. Their self-reliant philosophies got them into trouble in the early church.

My own Pelagian tendencies have gotten me in trouble, too. Sometimes I try to do far too much on my own and forget to call on God for help. I get burned out when I think that mapping my own life's course is only up to me. Thankfully, God is very persistent in the face of my stubbornness and reluctance to trust. God doesn't give up.

Scripture provides all kinds of examples of God's persistence in the face of human reluctance or obtuseness. I find comfort in the fact that, in the Old Testament, Samuel had to be awakened three times before he recognized that God was calling him. Each time he heard God's voice, Samuel thought he was hearing somebody else. It was a long time before he recognized God and finally said, "Speak, Lord, for your servant is listening."

The prophet Jeremiah, too, required some extra prodding from a persistent God. The first time he was called to be a "prophet to the nations" he gave the excuse of being too young to do all that was expected of him. He said to God, "Truly I do not know how to speak, for I am only a boy."

Sarah, on the other hand, in the book of Genesis, protested that she was too old to do what God asked of her. When God told her that she would have a child in her old age, she laughed. Sometimes what God asks of us seems too crazy. We laugh. Yeah, right! We shake our heads in self-doubt. We offer all kinds of excuses: we're too young, too busy, too afraid to answer God's call. Yet despite our excuses, God continues to invite us.

There have been plenty of times I have ignored God's call and have given a busy signal to God. One situation in particular stands out in my mind — God calling me to a relationship with my friend Jim. Jim was an old friend of mine from college whom I always kept in touch with after we graduated. During the years after college our communication was sporadic. We e-mailed each other every once in a while, and very rarely we would write letters and talk on the phone. We had the same group of friends in college, so occasionally I would see him at football games or at New Year's parties. Every time we would get back in touch with one another I was struck by the ease with which we communicated. We always just seemed to be in sync and had similar opinions on a whole host of issues. I noticed how other-centered he was, always thinking of how he could reach out to his friends and family and the other people in his life. There was something almost unidentifiable about

Jim that commanded respect. I always had admired him — for his personal integrity, for the profession he had chosen.

From time to time, I considered the possibility of dating him, but I could always think of excuses why it wouldn't work: we didn't live in the same city, we had different interests, we were both dating other people, and besides, he had the proverbial "just a friend" status.

But over the years a nagging feeling always rode on the tails of our correspondence. It was like a little person was pulling on my shirttail asking me from time to time: "What if?" "What is it about him that you just can't shake?" Somehow I felt that thoughts of Jim never quite left my consciousness.

Though I could sense a tug in my heart, I couldn't articulate very clearly in my head exactly what was going on at the time. Besides, there were too many practical considerations that I thought would prevent us from dating. I ignored the question.

I coincidentally ended up moving to a city that was about an hour away from where he lived. We got to see each other more often since we had many mutual friends. It was during these frequent visits and get-togethers with our friends that I realized that this was the person I wanted to be with, the person I wanted to date. I realized that we had to talk about our feelings for one another.

Acknowledging that there were feelings between the two of us was simultaneously both the scariest and most exciting thing I had ever done. To reveal my feelings to someone whom I knew was capable of understanding them in all their fullness was terrifying. I worried that any discussion that did not go well would permanently end our friendship. But as terrifying as it was to talk to Jim, it was a very good thing to do. It was the right and fair thing to do. At the same time, I wouldn't want to go through it all again! Looking back now, I can see that this may have been a case where God was calling me for a long time to take a serious look at my relationship with Jim. I am very grateful for God's persistence, because it took me a few years to figure this out.

Discussing my relationship with Jim had to be done. It was the right thing to do, even though it was difficult and intimidating to think about. I felt that talking to Jim was something that I couldn't *not* do. Parker Palmer, writing about vocation in *Let Your Life Speak*, states that vocation, at the core, is not "Oh, boy, do I want to go to this strange place where I have to learn a new way to live and where no one, including me, understands what I'm doing." Vocation at its deepest level, says Palmer, is to say, "This is something I can't not do, for reasons I'm unable to explain to anyone else and don't fully understand myself but that are nonetheless compelling." A call is, as Jesuit Father James Martin describes in his book *In Good Company,* "a happy inability to think of anything else."

Responding to the call of vocation can be very scary and completely unnerving. It may require us to do things that make no sense to other people and make very little sense to us. Yet we may feel compelled to make certain choices and decisions, even in the face of fear and other practical considerations. This compulsion comes from the deep sense that we were *made* for the life we are choosing, even if ensuing consequences are difficult. We can't *not* do it.

Finding Your Passion

These compelling feelings can be referred to as our passion. To discover your vocation is to discover your passion. Passion is something that takes hold of us, sometimes for reasons we can't explain. Sr. Helen Prejean, whose story of serving as a spiritual advisor to a death row inmate formed the basis for the book and movie *Dead Man Walking,* spoke of the importance of passion at my college graduation. Her last words to us, the graduating seniors, were these: "May you be blessed with passion, and may you follow it all of your life."

I like to pair Sr. Helen's words with those of Emily Dickinson, who wrote simply, "I dwell in possibility." Dickinson's words are hopeful words, portending great promise in what lies ahead. Both Prejean and Dickinson spoke words of hope, words ready to take on the future. Living the life that God calls us to live means to follow our passion, to live in possibility, to cast a hopeful eye to the future.

My friend Laura found the gift of passion in both her love of and her talent for music. She has felt that her passion, music, pursued *her* as much as she pursued music. After graduating from college, she decided to follow a career as an opera singer, a career that she describes as a vocation. She said to me, "I actually planned on being something way more practical but music followed *me,* nonetheless." Her chosen career presents no small number of lifestyle challenges, which often result in people saying to her, "I don't see how you can live like that!" Even wise and seasoned people within the opera profession itself say to her, "If you can imagine yourself doing anything else, do it."

"It didn't take me long to understand their perspective," said Laura, "for it is a very difficult career." Opera singing is not just a job — it is a lifestyle. The singing roles she takes on determine every other factor in her life for the time being: her geographical location, her peer group, her living situation. Work is limited and competition is fierce, guaranteeing that rejection is a continuous part of everyday life. In addition, opera singers who are successful rarely will be in the same place for more than a month or two at a time. Laura noted one of the ramifications of this: "This lifestyle makes it extremely difficult to have normal relationships with people, or to have a marriage and family without feeling like you are neglecting them."

"I have had to miss important family events, such as weddings and birthdays, because of a conflict with a singing engagement. I'm often faced with the hard choice of whether or not to give up an entire month's work for one day with family or friends." Laura described another difficulty, addressing the isolation that often accompanies a career as an opera singer: "It can be extremely lonely, and after a while it becomes easy to lose yourself or forget who you are."

In addition, opera is a profession in which the work is never done. "The amount of time I put into this career is endless," Laura said. "I'm constantly learning more roles, perfecting my vocal technique, improving my foreign languages, trying to stay healthy. It leaves little time for anything outside of opera, and can become overwhelming."

Yet even with all of the difficulties and challenges associated with being an opera singer, Laura finds very compelling reasons to keep pursuing the career. It is something she can't *not* do. "I do this because I love it, and I do feel fortunate to have a career that I love," she says. Laura has met many incredible people along the way, has traveled all over the world, and has experienced other cultures and traditions. She has been able to bring joy to a variety of people by sharing the gift of music.

Laura will tell you that she has learned much from the sometimes solitary nature of her career choice. "I really appreciate all the time I have spent alone because I feel that I understand myself better because of it. And truly, I don't know how long I will be lucky enough to pursue this career, so I am just enjoying every minute of its excitement!" Though Laura feels called to a particular career in music at this time, she recognizes that is something that may change. After a time, the transient nature of the lifestyle may wear on her and she may tire of missing out on time with her family.

This sentiment raises an important additional point about vocation: the particulars of one's vocation can change. There are some elements of our vocation that can be permanent, and some may be only temporary. We have "callings within callings," and what we feel called to at one point in our lives may change as we grow older, change geographic locations, grow in our faith, or respond to the needs of our community. Some callings may remain with us throughout our lives, but there will surely be variables that will change. Because of the dynamic nature of a vocation, listening for the voice of God is a lifelong pursuit. Truly living out our vocation means that we can never rest. Our vocation grows and changes as we grow and change, and because of this, discerning our vocation becomes a dynamic practice that we attend to throughout our lives.

Vocation Can Change

The other day I told one of the women I work with that I was writing a book. She asked me what it was about, and I talked to her about how I wanted to write the book for people in their twenties, especially for people who were concerned about the integration of faith and life choices. In a nutshell, I said, I wanted to write a book about vocation.

She nodded her head with approval. "Well, make sure you put something in there about the fact that vocation can change," she said to me thoughtfully. This wise and faith-filled woman, one of my favorite people, knows this very well. She has endured many vocational changes throughout her sixty years of life. She was a nun and lived in the convent for nearly fifteen years before deciding to leave when she was in her early thirties. She had begun to sense that she may be called to some other lifestyle. These initial thoughts of leaving the convent began in the midst of problems in the interpersonal relationships of her community. The conflicts began to wear on her, and in the throes of this rocky community life she began to notice what she describes as "the holiness and the goodness in the laypeople I worked with on a regular basis." She was impressed with the commitment and the joy with which her married friends lived. After lots of prayerful discernment, she decided to leave the convent life behind and began teaching at a Catholic high school. It was at the high school that she met the wonderful, faith-filled man she eventually married and had three children with.

"I don't think all of this meant that I never had a call to the convent," she says. "Life in the convent prepared me for a lot of things." It was the discipline and the prayer in which she rooted herself in the convent that kept her grounded when her husband died of cancer, leaving her to raise three children under the age of five. "I really felt that God wanted those children to be in the world," she said, "and that conviction has only grown as they have gotten older. And I am grateful for the six wonderful years I had with my husband."

In her sixty years she has embraced vocations to the religious life, the married life, and the single life. We attended a workshop together recently, and as we were filling out the registration forms, she joked that at different points in her life she could have checked off three different boxes: married, single, and religious! Anne exudes a particular incisiveness and wisdom because of the vocational changes she has endured. When I ask her for advice, I sense that I am consulting with someone who has *really* lived, someone who is truly faith-filled and has taken all of her decisions very seriously.

Not all of our vocational changes will be as dramatic as Anne's have been, but I do think that her life story illustrates that the specifics surrounding our vocation may change as we travel through life. Vocation encapsulates much more of who we are than whether we are married, single, or religious, but these categories are certainly an important element of our vocation. Few people will have the chance to live all three of these, but a life story like Anne's is indicative that we never know what God has in store for us, and we never know how our deepest desires will change. This is why listening and paying attention are so important: God can call us to make changes in the way we are living, and thus to discern a vocation means to respond to God's call daily and for the long haul. If we are close to God we are more attuned with the nuanced ways in which we are called.

There is a beautiful prayer that says, "Lord, help me find the *way* through the changes in my life" (emphasis added). Jesus said in John's Gospel, "I am the *way,* the truth, the life." The *way* in these two passages refers more to *who we are* than *what we do.* Who we are is always going to be bigger, more inclusive, more encompassing than what we do, though what we do certainly comprises a large portion of who we are. Though we may choose many different paths in life — sometimes we take those that branch off, sometimes those that loop around — the way that we follow can remain the same. The way is who we are; the path is what we do. Many paths can be included in one single way. If we find a way that we are comfortable with and stay true to, the changes in path won't disturb us as much. If we stay true to a way, the way will guide our choice of paths. Vocation is about following a way, and allowing that way to determine the paths we choose.

The discovery of a vocation involves some pretty weighty issues. I feel that I am just now beginning to see the proverbial tip of the iceberg in uncovering what vocation is all about. I do believe, though, that if I remember to listen, to pay attention, to remember that God is persistent, to remember that God will illuminate the way and lead me to choose the right paths, I will be able to find my true vocation and live it out in all its fullness. It will take time. It will probably take a lifetime. As the lyrics on the title track of an Indigo Girls CD remind us, "It takes a long, long time to become you."

 *Two*

Discernment

Asking the Big Questions

My Lord God, I have no idea where I am going.
I do not see the road ahead of me.
I cannot know for certain where it will end.
Nor do I really know myself, and the fact that I think that I
*   am following your will does not mean that I am actually*
*   doing so.*
But I believe that the desire to please you does in fact please
*   you,*
and I hope that I have that desire in all that I am doing.
I hope that I will never do anything apart from that desire.
And I know that if I do this, you will lead me by the right road
though I may know nothing about it.
Therefore I will trust you always
though I may seem lost and in the shadow of death.
I will not fear, for you are ever with me,
And you will never leave me to face my perils alone.

—Thomas Merton, *The Road Ahead*

It was a sunny Saturday afternoon, and I sat on my front porch, talking to a friend of mine who is in her late thirties. "I just wish I could get to a point in my life where there aren't any more transitions," I said. "I'm tired of circumstances changing all the time." My friend laughed and laughed, shaking her head at me. "Transition is a way of life, my friend," she said. "It's *always* going to be there." What she said reminded me of the old adage we have all heard again and again: "The only thing that is permanent in life is change."

I remember having a similar conversation about transition with my spiritual director a few months later. I spoke to her of both my enduring feelings of restlessness and my aggravation with life's mutability, but in a different way: "I wish I could just get caught up on everything in my life, I mean *really* caught up. I always feel so behind. Responsibilities pile up before I have a chance to even *think* about them and it drives me crazy. What do I do about this?" I asked her during our August meeting, as we sat in the late summer sun that filtered into her apartment windows.

She slowly nodded her head in agreement, as if to say, "I know exactly how you feel," and thoughtfully paused. I leaned forward and waited with bated breath to hear the secret to staying caught up in life. Surely, this wise woman, an earthy and elegant Franciscan sister in her sixties, would know. But her words surprised me. "By the time we all finally get caught up on everything we're supposed to," she said to me, shrugging her shoulders, "we're knocking on heaven's door." And that was pretty much it — that was this wise woman's final answer to my ramblings. In a nutshell, she was very nicely saying, "Just deal with it."

Change and transition are guaranteed to be a part of our lives for the long haul. This is a little daunting, since it seems that transitions rarely happen perfectly or easily. With every transition come adjustments, snags, shifts in perspective, and new challenges. Transitions require a lot from us in terms of our openness and energy.

Yet we continue to invite change into our lives. It seems that the dynamism of the human spirit does not lend itself very well to inertia. We continually grow, outgrow, change, and mature. It is in our very nature to both desire change and sometimes to resist it when it forces itself upon us. Maybe the challenge for us, then, is to grow in our acceptance of that dynamism and to face the test of transition with more trust and less trepidation.

Constant transition gives rise to the need for constant choice and steady decision-making on our part. Our generation has grown up in a culture of choice. Thanks to the steady march of human progress, we have an unprecedented number of choices of geographical location, career, educational opportunities, and products on which to spend our money.

For example, as a young woman, I have been given certain professional and recreational opportunities that were never available to my grandmother or even my mother. During my teenage years I chose to be a part of multiple girls' soccer teams: traveling, non-traveling, indoor, and outdoor. I eschewed hair ribbons and dresses in favor of shin guards and ponytails. I thought nothing of my multiple soccer pursuits; they were just what people my age did. It seemed like all of my friends played on more than one soccer team.

My mother and grandmother, on the other hand, were never encouraged to play sports at all. Girls' and women's soccer teams were unheard of during their childhoods. Athletic choices are just one example of how our lifestyle options have exceeded those of our forbears.

Other choices abound. Our generation has an unprecedented number of options with regard to geographical location, the availability of information, and consumer goods. With air travel being so commonplace, I can live in whatever part of the country I choose and still visit my family on a regular basis. With the advent and proliferation of the Internet, I can communicate with far more people than I ever could before. When I go to the grocery store I can count at least fifteen varieties of cream cheese to choose from: plain, strawberry, chive-and-onion, fat-free chive-and-onion, and so on. And in the future, our generation will have even more choices and options. Each of these options will require us to make decisions — many of them more significant than deciding what kind of cream cheese to purchase.

We're going to find ourselves at a variety of personal and professional crossroads throughout our lives. Every crossroads we reach requires a decision, a path to be discerned. As young adults we are faced with the little decisions and the big ones. The little ones aren't too bad: where to take your car so you get the best deal on an oil change, what to fix for friends who are coming over for dinner, when to leave for work so you can stop for coffee on the way and still be on time. Those decisions can even be fun.

The big decisions, on the other hand, can lead to a whole lot of stress and a world of heartache. There's a lot riding on who we choose as a life partner, *if* we decide to choose a life partner, what city we move to, which job or career path we settle into for the time being, how we are going to engage in public service and respond to national and world needs. All of these choices require extensive discernment.

Discernment is asking ourselves: What does God want me to do? How can I know for sure? Hello, God, anybody there? It's me again. What am I supposed to do this time? Should I accept this job offer? Should I end my relationship with this person? Where is this relationship going? Am I following the right career path? Am I working in a workplace that is just and fair? How am I to respond to the dire situations I see in the world around me? How can I find an occupation that both fulfills me personally and meets a need in society?

Discernment is a practice we undertake intentionally, a tool we pick up on purpose. To discern means to make a decision in the light of faith. It is a practice that can help us make decisions in our often overwhelming world. Discernment is a practice slightly more nuanced than scrawling and scribbling lists of pros and cons at the back of an old spiral notebook and seeing how they add up. Discernment is serious business and requires much of us in terms of time, energy, brainpower, and prayer.

Humanity has been making significant decisions for thousands of years. The ancient Greeks and Romans consulted oracles to help them decide what to do in certain situations. In biblical times, God sent all kinds of fascinating symbols and clues to hint (most of the time not so subtly) at what people's paths of action should be. Moses was stopped in his tracks by a burning bush. Mary received a surprise visit from an angel. Noah was given some very specific dimensions for building the ark. Sometimes I think that maybe the ancients had it easier. Who wouldn't pay attention to flaming shrubbery or a talking angel in their living room? The biblical folks had some very clear signs. But, then again, I remember that these stories were written down long after these events actually occurred, and, as we are often reminded, hindsight is always twenty-twenty. It is comforting, though, to recognize that thousands of faith-filled generations have undergone difficult decision-making processes and emerged not only unscathed, but as better people.

Joy and Happiness

In our own discernment process we may not receive such dramatic earthly signs as a burning bush or an angel. We can, however, look within ourselves for clues to help us make a big decision. One such clue is the inner joy that comes from making a good choice. "Inner joy" may seem to be an amorphous concept, the stuff of feel-good spiritualities and *Oprah* shows, but it is very real, and I would bet that you have felt it from time to time.

I used to think that joy and happiness were one and the same, but thanks to a few good mentors, I've discovered that there is an important distinction between the two. In fact, joy and happiness do not even always coincide. Joy, according to theologian Fr. Michael Himes, is not the same thing as happiness. Joy is a much deeper, more substantive conviction. Happiness, on the other hand, is dependent upon a thousand external circumstances: whether or not I've had a good night's sleep, if I had an argument with my mom on the phone last night, if my car is working right, or if I'm feeling healthy. Joy, on the other hand, is the inner conviction that what I'm doing is good even if it does not make me happy or content one hundred percent of the time. Joy is connected with a profound sense of conviction that this is a good way to live a life. Whether or not a certain person, job, lifestyle, or geographical location is a source of joy to you is of immense significance for your vocation. If a decision does not give you at least some semblance of inner joy it may be the case that that decision is not one you are called to make.

When I consider Fr. Himes's distinction between joy and happiness and how this distinction pertains to discernment, I think back to my graduate school internship at a large residential home-less shelter. My internship responsibilities simply were to spend time with the residents in the single women's dormitory and to lead them in a thoughtful fifteen-minute reflection and discussion before "lights out" at ten o'clock. The reflections had to do with inspirational topics like inner strength, faith, perseverance, and friendship. I had never worked with the homeless population before, and I was very much looking forward to the experience. I familiarized myself with all the stories and discussions in the three-ring binder of reflections and planned to drive to the shelter with a friend of mine every Tuesday night. I thought I was all set.

For the first six months those Tuesday nights were miserable. I felt, week after week, as if I were sitting in someone's living room uninvited. Every time I visited the women's dorm the guests walked back and forth past me repeatedly, not even acknowledging that I was there. "How dare they," I thought to myself. "Don't they know I am here to help and inspire them? When are they going to start appreciating me?"

The women's living quarters comprised two rooms: a living room area and a sleeping area. When I announced the evening reflections, not a single woman was interested in coming out to the living area to participate. They all stayed in the sleeping area and didn't even acknowledge my presence.

I began to wonder why I was putting the time into preparing these evening reflections. I began to think I had chosen the wrong internship. Of all the internship options in that little blue handbook that my program director had given me, why did I choose this one? Why didn't I sign up to work in a hospital or on a college campus with people who had a background more similar to mine? Was it too late to change internships? Was my lack of success going to sabotage my performance in my graduate program?

I struggled with these questions for weeks, but for some reason I hung in there — probably because I was too embarrassed to tell my supervisor that things just weren't working out, that these women just didn't like me, that I wasn't really a "people person" after all, as I had claimed to be. But for some reason I did choose to stay at the homeless shelter and eventually, almost imperceptibly, the tenor of my experience began to change.

It would start when one woman would say a few words to me as we sat in the living room area watching television together. Then someone else would ask me, "What was your name again, girl?" And someone else would tell me a little bit about her day, about how she was doing everything she could to regain custody of her kids, or about how she had two job interviews tomorrow. Then some of the women stayed in the living room area for the evening reflections instead of going straight to bed. For many months, months that eventually stretched into two years, we shared our thoughts on freedom, strength, forgiveness, and healing.

These women turned out to be a wealth of information on life's lessons. They told me that if I were ever having a bad day I should wear the color purple because it is the color of strength. One night we even shared a sign of peace, which eventually became a regular practice. These women and I ended up building a beautiful relationship, one of trust, support, and depth.

Though our relationship grew, the discomforts certainly didn't go away. I still ran out of things to talk about with them sometimes, and occasionally I felt as if they were doing and saying things just to shock me. "I just took ten Tylenol," my friend Cindy said to me proudly one evening. "I'm getting outta here. Tomorrow I'm leaving on a bus to Arkansas," said another woman. The guests at the shelter came and went, and many nights I arrived there immediately disappointed to learn that one of my "favorites" had been asked to leave the shelter or had moved out.

Even with all the difficulties and discomforts, each time I drove away from that homeless shelter I was so glad I had gone. I felt like I had a seat by a window opening into some of the most beautiful souls — wounded souls and deeply spiritual souls that were in desperate need of healing, souls that were incredibly open and receptive to God, though I don't know if they would have ever phrased it that way. I remember sharing my experiences there with some of my friends and recall saying on a number of occasions, "I can't imagine a better way to spend my time." And I really meant it. My experiences at the center for the homeless provided me with a deep sense of inner joy.

I came away from the experience with a deeper understanding of humanity and my own place within it. I realized that I was both richer than I'd thought, in some ways, and poorer than I had thought, in others. The insights I developed, however, were not always very explicit. I only grabbed glimpses of them, in between nights like the one when all the women sat captivated by the *Top Ten Car Crashes* show on Fox Television and could care less if I were there.

My internship at the homeless shelter didn't always make me happy, but it certainly was a source of joy. It was such a source of joy that I ended up working there even after my internship was finished. I was tested at the shelter, but in such a way that it demanded more of me than superficial happiness. In situations that require discernment, it always helps to try and distinguish between what is a source of happiness and what is a wellspring of joy.

I've found that sometimes, when faced with a decision, the best thing to do is to reflect on what has given you joy in the past. There may be some hints in your past experiences as to what will give you joy in the future. I will continue to look back on this experience at the homeless shelter, especially when I find myself in a professional situation that is less than ideal. I will remember what it was like to be challenged in a way that my happiness was threatened, but my joy was not. Ideally, happiness and joy go hand-in-hand, and when they have, I have felt as if I were walking on water, imbued with a sense that all is somehow right in the world. I felt that sense of rightness on some days at the shelter, and that sense was sufficient to carry me through the more difficult days there.

I wish I could share with you that, now that I can better distinguish between happiness and joy, my personal discernment process always concludes with a resounding internal, heartfelt "yes!" I wish I could tell you that, after a period of conscientious discernment, I reach a definitive conclusion and jump up triumphantly, like in the old deodorant commercial that says "raise your hand if you're SURE." Though in discernment we may yearn for that "aha!" moment, it has been my experience thus far that discernment rarely leads to absolute certainty or an ultimate moment of clarity.

Discernment certainly requires us to trust in God and take a leap of faith. But discernment also requires us to do some work. It is important, first, to reflect on previous decisions that have given us joy and past situations that have provided us with a sense of joy and fulfillment. Second, we need to gather the data. Gathering the data is just as important as undertaking our discernment in a spirit of prayer. Discernment always requires practical considerations just as much as it does spiritual considerations.

So, for example, if you are considering a particular career, consult the experts, people who have pursued the career path you are interested in. Find out how they support themselves. Ask them about their benefits, the hours, the pitfalls and advantages of their chosen careers. Gather as much data as you can. If you are considering choosing a particular person as a life partner, gathering the data is just as important. Spend as much time with that person's family as you can. How do you feel about that person's family? Could you see yourself as a member of that family, spending holidays with them, getting through difficult times with them? Reflect on your life partner's chosen profession. Are you comfortable with that person's career and do you understand any of the ramifications it may have for the two of you, financially, geographically, spiritually, and emotionally?

The list of practical questions can be endless. In any discernment process, a very natural first step is to gather the data. Visit the city you want to move to. Talk to people who are working in a profession you are considering. Read books by people you admire. Log onto the Internet and check out the websites of the educational institutions you are curious about. Much of the stress that accompanies difficult decisions can be alleviated simply by gathering some practical data. Good, thorough, thoughtful discernment should be both prayerful and practical. Gathering the data will help you to get the process off to a good start.

The Point of No Return

The whole point of discernment as a practice is that it should eventually lead us to action. Ultimately we reach the point in our discernment process when we make our best guess and act. I remember during my final semester of graduate school I was trying to decide between two job offers in two different states. Both jobs had qualities I liked, but I could not decide between the two. I fretted and worried that I would make the wrong decision. What if I made a mess of my entire future career path by choosing the wrong job?

My boss where I was working at the time told me not to accept either job. She told me to wait things out and keep an eye out for something better that would surely come along. My friends helped me weigh the pros and cons, and I did everything short of writing them all out on a piece of paper. I cried and worried, I prayed, and I rented movies that I thought would inspire me sufficiently enough to make the right decision. I thought I was doomed. In my frustration with my indecision I somehow convinced myself that I was destined to be unemployed, that I had chosen the wrong career, that I had wasted three years on a graduate degree I would never use.

But just when I thought I had reached a total impasse, the most subtle variable had a surprising impact. What tipped me over the edge, away from my uncertainty and into a decision, was a casual comment from my father. "You know, what if you asked for a little more money from the one job and negotiated a few of your responsibilities? That first job you were offered actually sounded pretty good to me." His suggestion was just the little nudge I needed. Though I was by no means absolutely certain that this was the job for me, I had had a very good interview experience there, and it sounded good enough when coupled with a little recommendation from someone I really trusted. I am now finishing my second year at that job and will probably stay for a third. I certainly don't love it every day, and there are things about it that drive me crazy, but I am very glad to work where I work, and am grateful to have a job that I love most days.

In the process of discernment it often helps to consult with the people we love, trust, and admire. Though ultimately we're the ones who have to make the decision, we don't make decisions in a vacuum. A decision we make is like throwing a stone into a lake. It causes ripples that move outward in concentric circles, beginning with the people closest to us, geographically and emotionally. Our choices affect our family relationships, our friendships, and our professional networks. One of my mentors once warned me how difficult it is to be a lone ranger decision-maker, to go at it alone and make a choice that isolates us from many of our support systems.

It is good to consult people who will give you their honest assessment of what you should do, even if it includes challenging words that are hard to hear. I've found that it is really difficult to follow a path when the majority of the people you love don't feel that you are following the right path. It does happen, though, that parents or friends may not understand when we choose a certain lifestyle or relationship. That is when it is important to really trust your gut and your heart, to listen within yourself for a solution.

Discernment requires us to listen within ourselves, to listen within the quiet of our hearts where our feelings are the deepest. Theologian Rev. John Dunne, C.S.C., calls this place our "center of stillness surrounded by silence." We can take other people's voices to heart, but ultimately, in the final stages of a decision, we have to listen within ourselves. This is difficult, because it is sometimes our own voice that is the hardest voice to trust.

For some reason we trust everyone else so much more than we trust ourselves, yet within our very own souls is where the key to discernment often resides. Quaker scholar Parker Palmer, in his book *Let Your Life Speak,* writes about the many retreats he has led, where participants show him the pages of notes they have written based on his talks. According to Palmer, the pattern is nearly always the same: people take lots and lots of notes on what the retreat leader says, and they sometimes jot down some of the clever comments from their co-retreatants, but rarely, if ever, do they write down their own thoughts from within. In this little story Palmer illustrates the hesitancy we all have sometimes to listen to ourselves. For whatever reason, everyone else seems to have more of a probability of being "right" than we do. Discernment can be a stressful, painful process, but when we listen within, it can be an exciting means to self-discovery. So don't be afraid to listen to yourself. Trust yourself. You know more than you think.

When people talk about good decisions they've made they often speak of a "gut feeling" that has helped guide them. I am a firm believer in gut feelings, and have relied on plenty of them myself over the years. It has only been recently that I've begun to identify the Holy Spirit as the source of those feelings. In my mind, a "gut feeling" is indicative of the presence of the Holy Spirit.

I attended a conference in Seattle where one of the keynote speakers, spiritual writer Edwina Gateley, affirmed that God was located approximately three inches inside of one's belly button. And I thought to myself: "Well, *that* theory accounts for those gut feelings then, and how convincing they are." It was the first time I had an inkling that a gut feeling had anything to do with the divine.

Gateley affirmed that God moves, breathes, and lives deep, deep within us. Deep within us is a place where our will and God's will come together. In the process of discernment it is important to trust that God is present within us. We know what we have to do most of the time, but we just have a hard time trusting our gut occasionally, especially when our heads are saying things like "It's too risky. . . . " "I could never say that. . . . " "I couldn't live there. . . . " Gut feelings are indicative of the presence of the Holy Spirit. Pay attention to them.

Focus on the Big Questions

It is common practice to agonize over painful decisions about our relationships, our jobs, our future. We convince ourselves that what we decide is going to affect us for the rest of our lives and could ultimately determine our eventual fulfillment or happiness. I've found that sometimes we waste time fretting over the little questions, when what we really should be doing is focusing on the big questions.

The other day I spoke with an acquaintance who works with young adult ministries in Chicago. We discussed some of the issues that young adults confront frequently, one of them being, "Will I ever be married?" While many of us ask this question, is it possible that the bigger question we're really asking ourselves is, "Will I be loved as an adult?" When we ask ourselves, "How long should I keep my current job?" we are really asking, "Is this job nurturing me personally and fulfilling a need in society?"

I can think of an example in my own life when I spent far too much time obsessing over the little questions instead of spending time reflecting on the bigger, more fundamental question. My boyfriend and I had been dating for six years, some of those years taking the form of a long-distance relationship. Eventually we were both able to find jobs in the same city, and everything was fine for a while. We developed a routine in which we were able to balance our jobs, our friends, and other interests. After about a year, however, my boyfriend applied to and was accepted at a medical school in a city almost two hundred miles away from where we were both living.

I agonized over whether I would move when he moved. I thought about all the possible career angles for me and about the city's proximity to my family. I came up with a few possible scenarios under which living in that city would benefit me professionally. I eventually decided that I would move there as long as all of my qualifications were met, as long as certain professional opportunities fell into place, as long as I could find a good place to live.

I realize now, the relationship since ended, that during that time of discernment I concerned myself too much with the smaller question, my career opportunities. Potential career opportunities were a very important consideration, but the bigger question was "Is this relationship worth enough to me that I will make important sacrifices for it, that is, do I really love this person?" Had we as a couple spent more time discerning this bigger question, I think we both could have saved ourselves a lot of heartache and tears.

The same preoccupation with little questions can happen in the discernment of a career. We can get caught up in asking ourselves what city we want to live in or who we'll live with, when the more significant question is: What kind of work do I feel called to do? What kind of needs are there in the working world and where do my talents fulfill those needs? It may take weeks, months, a lifetime to answer those big questions but we need to keep chipping away at them, continuing the discernment process. That is what vocation is about — continually questioning, asking the big questions over and over again.

A contemporary European monk, Dom Andre Louf, cannily expresses the importance of revisiting big questions as the idea pertains to his life as a monk. He writes,

> What is a monk?
> A monk is someone who every day asks:
> "What is a monk?"

According to Louf's incisive words, a good monk is a monk who continually questions. In turn, the way we live the life God is calling us to live is continually to ask, "How do I think God is calling me to live in this world?" That question is fundamental and is worth spending a lifetime discerning. Big questions like these consume our hearts and minds, questions that do not go away even when we try to ignore them. Though I still have a way to go in mastering this practice, I've at least gained enough awareness to recognize when I am wasting my energy on the little questions.

Have a Heart-to-Heart with God

The practice of discernment is best undertaken in a spirit of prayer. Prayer is the bedrock of discernment and decision-making. Prayer, most simply defined, is a heart-to-heart conversation with God. We all have our conversations with God in different ways, at different times, and in different languages. What matters is not *how* we talk to God, but that we *do* talk to God, and allow God to speak to us. What is most important is that we simply have conversation with God on a regular basis.

Nourishing our relationship with God is like nurturing a good friendship. It takes time and effort for good communication and understanding to develop. Eventually we reach a point in a good relationship where words are not always necessary. We can simply rest in another person's presence, communicating with that person in more subtle ways.

Rev. William Toohey, C.S.C., a Holy Cross priest who died in the 1980s, shared in an article a wonderful story that illustrates the importance of conversation quite poignantly. He wrote of his observation of his parents' marital relationship and how it deepened and grew over time. He described in his article the way in which his parents used to sit across from one another in the living room after dinner each evening. His father would read the *Saturday Evening Post* and his mother would darn socks, knit, or read. They sat there in silence, absorbed in their pursuits, for an hour or so. After a while, his mother would grow restless, fold up her knitting, and begin to putter around the house. As soon as she was out of her chair his father's newspaper went down immediately. "Where are you going?" he would ask, obviously disappointed. "Don't get excited," she would answer. "I'm just going out to the kitchen."

Though his parents were exchanging no words, his father was very conscious of his mother's presence and found comfort and peace with her in the living room. This couple had laid the foundation, through many years of marriage, for this kind of communication, that of simply resting in each other's presence. For days that stretched into months that stretched into years, by continually conversing, probably many times about very mundane things, they had built up to this level of communication that allowed them to simply rest in and be aware of each other's presence.

Much of our conversation begins at the stage of small talk and basic questions. Fr. Toohey writes:

> Although some people remain on this conversational level for a lifetime, most of us experience the progress that accompanies a developing friendship, and are very grateful for it. For most of us, conversation rather quickly becomes more spontaneous, informal, personal, and honest. We don't worry so much about what to say; we begin to share our

deepest thoughts and feelings; and, eventually, we find that we're perfectly comfortable not saying a word, content to appreciate each other's presence.

I have been fortunate to reach this level of communication in some of my own friendships. There are some treasured friendships in which we do not always have to be engaged in conversation. After many years of friendship, communication can take other forms. I have noticed lately that my friend Emily and I seem to have reached this level. We have been friends for ten years, and I am just now beginning to realize the value of a friend who has known me for a long time. ("Hang on to friends who have known you since you were young," says my favorite newspaper columnist, "because you'll value them when you are old.")

I spent a holiday weekend at Emily's house recently and we went to all the usual places: bars, restaurants, movies, and (late) Mass on Sunday. Then Sunday afternoon rolled around. Emily wanted to stay at home and do some yardwork, so I helped her weed for a while and then decided to read a book on her deck. For two hours I sat and read while she leisurely weeded her garden. We spoke very little but there was something very comforting and relaxing about that Sunday afternoon.

I know that we never would have spent an afternoon that way as college sophomores — we would have spent that two hours *doing* something, probably engaged in conversation the entire time. We still have good conversations, but we are at that point in our friendship where we don't have to talk all the time. It took us years to get to that point — years of getting to know each other's families, taking classes together, traveling together to visit friends, working through each other's problems, and just being there for each other when we were needed.

Our relationship with God works the same way. We may begin our conversations with the rote memorization of prayers that we learned as children. These rote prayers may work just fine for a while and then, eventually we may combine them with a more conversational style of prayer. At some point we may be comfortable sitting in silence, just listening to God in the quiet of our hearts. It may take a while to get to that point. But it is much easier to ask God for help with our decisions when the personal relationship is already there.

Laying a foundation for conversation with God is an important practice for discernment. I think of it kind of like playing baseball. It is hard to show up and hit a home run on game day when you haven't been to any of the practices. It is impossible to run a marathon (at least nearly impossible) unless one has trained for a few months. Like in any pursuit, slow, steady, regular efforts are necessary.

The practice of discernment is ongoing and lifelong. That is why staying in touch with God along the way is so important. Though we may find answers to our little questions, big questions will always remain. Through the practice of discernment, we will find answers to our questions. When we get *an* answer, however, we should not confuse it with *the* answer. Circumstances and situations will change enough throughout our lives that we will continually have to revisit those big questions, so it is good to develop good decision-making habits now.

❧ *Three* ❧

Stop Signs

Rejections, Failures, Mistakes, and Limits

To reach something good it is very useful to have gone astray, and thus acquire experience. —St. Teresa of Avila

It is hidden all the way in the back of my metal file cabinet, in the darkest, dustiest corner. It is the file folder whose contents I look at only when I have to. The pile of papers is quite thick, and I can feel its heft every time I pick it up for one reason or another. It is my "rejection file," similar to the "wall of shame" many college seniors construct, where they post their rejection letters from educational institutions or businesses for all in the dorm to see. Walls of shame and rejection files both serve the same purpose. They pay tribute to our failures. They pay humble homage to our shortcomings.

My rejection file is the packet of cumulative "no's" that I have received from schools, potential employers, and competition sponsors over the years. The sheaf of form letters includes phrases that fly like arrows into the ego: "Dear Ms. LaReau, we regret to inform you that . . . " and "unfortunately we have hired someone with more experience" and "the number of quality essays that were submitted made it extremely difficult to choose a winner" and "we will keep your application on file in case . . ." and, worst of all, "your article lacks emotional resonance." Sometimes these phrases are tempered with a hopeful "keep us in mind for the future," but it hardly helps. A rejection is a rejection. No means no.

The generic and formal wording in the text of such correspondence does little to soothe the wounded ego. Though the surface level sentiments are polite, the subliminal message of these letters is clear: We don't want you. We don't need you right now. We found someone else whom we prefer over you, at least for the time being. Your skills and talents are not enough for us. You are not adequate. Try again next time.

I am not sure exactly why I keep this rejection-filled file folder. It is certainly humbling to flip through the thick sheaf of papers. The file reminds me that for every "yes" I've been granted in my life, there has been a formidable stack of "no's" that has preceded it. For every job offer I have received there have been two or three rejections. For every article I have gotten published there has been one that I have not been able to place anywhere. I have yet to win an essay contest. It has been my experience that typically a host of negative responses serve as a precursor to one single affirmative response.

My rejection file is an ink-and-paper call to humility — perhaps that is one of the reasons I save it. It reminds me that one does not often get somewhere without first going nowhere for a while. It reminds me that I am still traveling up the steep part of life's learning curve. The sense of humility that the rejection file brings provides a good sense of perspective. I have a lot to learn.

At the same time, however, I think part of the reason I keep my rejections is so someday, at some as yet undesignated future time when I have "made it" in my career, I can go back and shake these papers in their authors' faces (or at least dream about it!) saying "Do you see?" "Do you see what you missed out on?" "I was a *catch!*" I am not-so-subtly hoping that I will, later on in life, turn into something that these people, my denunciators, would see as desirable. As one of my friends is known to say in the face of rejection: "Let's face it, you guys. This is all about pride, plain and simple." I save the rejection file, thinking that one day it will help me to reclaim some of my pride. And so every time I look at the file I dutifully put it back in its rightful place, in the darkest corner of the file cabinet.

Rejection is tough. Failure stinks, to say it nicely. Mistakes humble us. Limits provoke feelings of inadequacy and vulnerability. But unfortunately, as we know all too well already, all of these setbacks are an integral part of the package that life delivers to our doorsteps. In addition, they play a significant role in our vocational journey. Rejections and mistakes are difficult to endure, yet we all seem to have a story of curse-turned-blessing or setback-turned-opportunity. I have watched many *Today Show* or *Good Morning America* guests, featured and interviewed because of their latest movie, book, or other accomplishment, who have spoken fondly of their setbacks and initial rejections. One successful magazine editor spoke of "climbing up a mountain of 'no's' to reach the top, where she finally was granted that one pivotal 'yes.'" This magazine editor is not alone in this experience. Usually, in the lives of those who have been successful, there have been many rejections, mistakes, and regrets. Very, very few of us lead such a charmed life that we do not have to endure these setbacks in large doses.

Our shortcomings play a role in the cultivation of our vocation that is absolutely critical. Our obstacles are just as important as our opportunities. It may be our mistakes and failures that open us up to meaningful relationships that will serve as future sources of challenge and encouragement. Our setbacks and rejections may cause us to choose alternative paths and different portals and doorways that lead us to interesting and fulfilling destinations. In the journey toward the discovery of our vocation, our failures become just as pivotal as our opportunities. The doors that close in our faces are as significant, if not more significant, than the doors that open and beckon us inside. Our rejections determine the course of our future just as much as the decisions that catapult us toward success.

I can think of many occasions in my own life when my rejections have been extremely pivotal in the cultivation of my own vocation. One example that comes to mind immediately took place when I auditioned for a spot as a flautist in the university orchestra as a college freshman. An orchestra is dominated by stringed instruments: violas, violins, cellos, and string basses. A typical orchestra holds very few slots for woodwind instruments. As a flautist, I was very aware that my chances were already slim. Knowing this, I was extremely nervous before my tryout with the conductor.

And my nervousness showed. I completely botched the musical audition, having chosen a piece of music that required technical sophistication that was far beyond my abilities. The whole experience was a nightmare. I even had to start the piece over again at one point. I left the audition knowing that I would not be selected for the orchestra. Though I knew the rejection was coming, I checked the selection list in the music building a few days later. I still was upset when I saw that my name was not listed in the flute section on the orchestra bulletin board, though I was hardly surprised.

After the rejection from orchestra sunk in, I realized part of my dismay came from the fact that I felt I was losing a part of my identity. All my life until this point I had been known as an accomplished flautist and had been accepted in every ensemble for which I had auditioned. Now, however, that part of my personhood, my identity as an accomplished musician, was threatened. Playing the flute was a talent that many people associated with me. What would I do if I could not continue playing the flute in college?

I began to worry that I would not be able to find a musical niche on campus. I fretted that I would not be able to find a musical venue in which to play the classical music that had become so important to me. I searched the university handbooks and lists of activities and found a choir that I could audition for, a choir that utilized instrumentalists in their music for Sunday Mass at the beautiful, enormous church on campus. I was up for anything. I just really wanted to find a group with whom I would be able to play my flute.

I auditioned with the director and was accepted into the choir. Though I wasn't crazy about the musical group during my first year, I gradually, unexpectedly fell in love with the whole experience. My participation with the choir has become, without a doubt, one of the most formative experiences of my life. I established friendships that I hope will be lifelong relationships and, along with the forty other musicians, toured different parts of the country for a variety of performances.

But perhaps the most valuable and profound part of my experience was the way it changed the way I looked at my musical abilities. I used to look at playing the flute from the vantage point of performance. The only "real" music, in my opinion, was classical music, not the simple, singable tunes I heard at church. Those songs were stiff, banal, and preachy.

But everything changed, gradually, when I began to play the flute at Mass. I began to look upon playing the flute as a ministry, a service to other people. I started to realize that music touches hearts and souls in a way that spoken words cannot. I began to familiarize myself with the enormous repertoire of music that the church has acquired, rich with symbol, image, history, and meaning. I learned that there was a patron saint of music, St. Cecilia. I recalled words I had learned during my childhood years: "When you sing you pray twice." Somehow I really grew to believe the truth behind those words. I felt that truth in my heart. Music was prayer.

At Mass, from my perch in the choir loft behind my music stand and microphone, I began to look for the color changes in banners and vestments during the seasons of the church year. I felt as though a whole new world had been opened to me, a whole new way of keeping time. Music and faith became intertwined in a way that they never had before. I realized that there is a tremendous richness in the seasons, readings, and musical repertoire of the church. I realized that music was not solely a performance but a ministry to be shared with others. I came to the slow realization that I had a vocation as a musician.

This giant shift in consciousness has been a tremendous gift in my life. Though my initial rejection from the orchestra was difficult to swallow, I now hate to think what would have happened if I had never been a part of a college choir. Things would be very different now. Everything probably would have turned out okay, but at this point, I'm very, very grateful the orchestra conductor rejected me. One door closed and a window opened — a window into a beautiful, musical, spiritual landscape I never knew existed. I found a landscape where I could do something that I loved and serve others at the same time. All these blessings were the result of a rejection.

Rejection hurts. Many times, however, rejection is not merely a stop sign, but an invitation to a different opportunity. In my own life, failure has been a pivotal part of the discovery of my own vocation as a musician. In other words, there is hope on the other side of our obstacles. What would have become of Galileo if he had listened to the institutional church's admonition that he had incorrectly described the movements of the cosmos? What would have happened to Jesus' disciples if Jesus had given up on them the first time they had shown the slightest bit of misunderstanding or obtuseness? Would Catherine of Siena be known as "St. Catherine of Siena" today if she had listened to criticisms of her extensive travel or critical remarks about her call for women to refuse rejections? Would Hagar, the Egyptian slave girl in the book of Genesis, have relied so heavily on God had she not been emotionally broken down by the disparaging treatment by Abraham and the barren Sarah? What would our world be like if these tremendous individuals had not seen the hope on the other side of their setbacks? Certainly these people have enriched our world with their examples, lives characterized by strength and perseverance despite difficult odds.

What other human examples may we have lost had they not persevered in the face of criticism? Our history holds hundreds of stories of those who owe much of their success to their setbacks. Mistakes, obstacles, failures, and rejections are just as much a part of the human experience as are our virtues and triumphs. Often, one seemingly insurmountable obstacle will change the course of one's entire life. Thus, in a discussion of vocation it is good to spend a fair amount of time addressing these "negativities" and the role they play in our vocational journeys.

The Flip Side

One of the fundamental skills one develops in college chemistry classes is the ability to identify the rate-limiting step in a chemical equation, that is, the slowest part of a chemical reaction. The speed of the entire chemical reaction is reduced to whatever the speed of the rate-limiting step is. Burgeoning chemists learn early on that certain compounds have high melting points and particular elements have unique characteristics that require very specific environmental conditions in order to react with other elements.

We all are wired with our own rate-limiting steps, our own slowest parts. It is our shortcomings just as much as our gifts and talents that determine the rate at which we are able to accomplish things. It is our faults just as much as our virtues that determine the quality of our interactions with others. It is our limits just as much as our charisms that determine the strength of our character. We are, sometimes, only as good, only as effective as our slowest part, our rate-limiting step. Our rate-limiting steps are just as much an integral part of us as our gifts.

I have no trouble identifying my number one rate-limiting step, my largest personal "stop sign," which often brings my pursuit of greatness to a crashing halt. I am, much of the time, as impatient as they come. I am often the first to grow restless at work-related meetings. When our staff meetings run longer than their usual duration of one hour, I fidget and curb my comments so that we can adjourn as soon as possible. I do this even when my opinions are needed in a discussion. In one-on-one tête-à-têtes, I often verbally interrupt long-winded people by making a brusque comment or two. In the car I have run more yellow (and yellow-turned-red) traffic lights than I have ever stopped for. (I was mildly miffed when I read in my local newspaper that the city would soon install hidden cameras in all traffic signals to catch and punish people like me.) I have sometimes hurt friends with my curt comments, many of them born of impatience.

Patience is a virtue, as they say, and I know that I do not have enough of it. My lack of patience is my primary rate-limiting step. No matter how much I work at cultivating more patience, the ugly monster that is my abundance of impatience continues to rear its unsightly head much more often than I would like.

There is a flip side to my impatience, however. Impatience does have its privileges. Because of my impatience I am very good at meeting deadlines. I can be very efficient in the completion of a professional task that is given to me. My impatience often leads me to be more honest with people who have hurt me or disappointed me and prevents me from dishonestly sugar-coating my opinions. (Some people appreciate that kind of honesty, and some definitely do not.) Though I have to continue to work at acquiring more patience, I also recognize that there is a flip side to my impatience, a more positive side. Our limits are not all bad. Sometimes they are just our best traits in excess, or our virtues taken to an extreme.

Our limits all have a flip side that can be put to good use. In addition, our limits can often actually foster creativity, that wonderful human mechanism that often is galvanized by difficult circumstances. When we have a limited quantity of virtue, talent, or skill, this limitation forces us to compensate for our shortcomings in alternative, creative ways. Our limits often force us to find alternative ways of living.

David Sedaris, a regular contributor to Public Radio International's *This American Life,* is an example, if an irreverent one, of how our limits can foster creativity. In his semi-autobiographical book *Me Talk Pretty One Day,* he describes his battle with a speech impediment in the form of a sibilant "s," which meant that he lisped. When he spoke, "Sorry" became "Thorry," and "colleges and universities" became "collegeth and univerthitieth." Well-meaning teachers enrolled Sedaris in speech therapy programs at his elementary school. He worked with a speech therapist at the end of the school day for a number of months with no discernible improvement. Eventually his lack of progress discouraged him, and he looked for alternatives to the speech therapy classes that he despised.

To compensate for his lisp, he decided to develop an alternative vocabulary, one that included no "s" words at all. He describes his new approach to speech in this way:

> I tried to avoid an *s* sound whenever possible. "Yes," became "correct," or a military "affirmative." "Please," became "with your kind permission," and questions were pleaded rather than asked. After a few weeks of what she called "endless pestering" and what I called "repeated badgering," my mother bought me a pocket thesaurus, which provided me with *s*-free alternatives to just about everything. I consulted

the book both at home in my room and at the daily learning academy other people called our school.... The majority of my teachers were delighted. "What a nice vocabulary," they said. "My goodness, such big words!"

Therein lies a witty example of someone who took a lemon and quite innovatively made lemonade. Our limits can foster creativity. No doubt this successful Public Radio International commentator — a wordsmith with a lisp and a huge vocabulary — would agree.

Mistakes and Failures

At the National Spelling Bee, which takes place in Washington, D.C., every year, school-age spellers from around the country gather for nearly a week of competition. One year, for days on end, two hundred jittery adolescents, myself included, sat nervously on the stage under hot lights at the Capital Hilton, numbered placards around our necks, as we spelled words for eight hours a day. Words like "diaphanous" and "connoisseur," "loquacious" and "elegiacal," buzzed through the air. After spelling a word, each contestant would wait expectantly for one of two sounds. Silence meant that one had spelled the word correctly. The sharp "ding" of a bell, however, meant that one had chosen the wrong vowel, inadvertently missed a consonant, or had otherwise misspelled the word in some way. Any speller who misspelled a word was kindly escorted off the giant stage. With each new day, the number of chairs on stage grew smaller and smaller as young spellers were gradually eliminated. Our young nerves, as yet untested by an experience such as this, grew more and more frazzled.

After two days of competition the judges exhausted the list of words we had all dutifully memorized and proceeded to choose words from the dictionary. We all started dropping like flies after the dreaded "dictionary rounds" began. I made it through one dictionary round by spelling "bienniums," hardly believing my stroke of luck that I had been given a word that was easy to sound out. But, in the next round I was given the word "terpsichore," which I spelled t-e-r-p-s-i-c-o-r-y. The dainty sound of a little bell promptly informed me that I had spelled the word incorrectly, and I was escorted off stage, as others before me had been, to a sympathetic chorus of applause from newspaper journalists and hundreds of spellers' families and friends.

I was immediately escorted to the "Comfort Room." This specially designated space (and yes, there was an official "Comfort Room" sign on the door) was set aside for eliminated spellers to reunite with their families. The comfort room was equipped with cold sodas, big boxes of Kleenex, and the largest dictionary I'd ever seen. (As if I would want to pour salt on my wound by looking at that horrible t-word again.) I sobbed and sobbed when I reached the comfort room. I didn't win the spelling bee. The fun was over. There were spellers onstage who were better than me. I was crushed.

My already-fragile adolescent eighth grade ego suffered a great blow. Never mind that, in months of previous competitions, I had triumphantly mastered words like "shillibeer" and "septuagenarian," "aberration" and "armaments." All I could think of is that I had not spelled "terpsichore" correctly. I had made a huge mistake.

The very establishment of a comfort room at an event like the National Spelling Bee is just one small sign of how deeply our mistakes can wound us. The spelling bee organizers knew how upsetting mistakes can be, especially to young people. The very fact that there is a specially designated room for "losers" speaks volumes about how our culture views mistakes. Blessed are the losers, for they shall be comforted in a special room!

The impression left by our mistakes and failures is sometimes more lasting than that left by our successes, accomplishments, and triumphs. Often at the end of a workday we quickly forget all the tasks we have performed correctly or the many times we have helped someone. What sticks with us, for some reason, are the times we put our foot in our mouths or the time we were corrected by a co-worker or boss. Mistakes can really humble us and can severely bruise the ego, even though many of us have been taught since the time we were six years old that "Everyone makes mistakes." Mistakes leave a lasting impression.

Mistakes, failures, and obstacles are painful, but of course, we can learn a lot from them if we allow ourselves. One of the most powerful and best-loved stories in Scripture tells of a son who made the enormous mistake of leaving home and greedily squandering his inheritance while enjoying the pleasures of wine, women, and song for an extended period of time.

After spending his entire inheritance, the prodigal son loses all sense of human dignity, saying to himself, "How many of my father's hired men have all the food they want and more, and here am I dying of hunger! I will leave this place and go to my father and say: 'Father, I have sinned against you; I no longer deserve to be called your son.'" This acknowledgment of sinfulness, this stripping away of pride, is what in turn reopens the prodigal son to his father's love. It took a mistake of significant magnitude to communicate to him how very much his father loved him. It took a mistake to make him vulnerable, aware of and open to his father's love.

The prodigal son's mistake resulted in great learning, in greater awareness, and the strengthening of a familial relationship. This powerful testament to the love of a father illustrates that our mistakes can open doors that lead to learning. Like they did for the prodigal son, our mistakes can also open doors to love. They humble us enough to open us to love that we were too proud to be receptive to before. Mistakes break down the barriers of self-sufficiency that we so often build up around us. Mistakes aren't all bad. Stories like that of the prodigal son remind us that they have a flip side. Mistakes, as far as they instill in us a sense of our own limitations, can open us up to learning and to love.

A Bite of Humble Pie

God loves us despite our limits. I think we all know this on a "head level" and would say that we believe it, but it is another thing to internalize this belief and to know it on a "soul level." We don't know anyone else who loves us this unconditionally and who forgives us so readily! St. Paul's letter to the Romans offers some very encouraging words with regard to the topic of our obstacles. He writes, "For I am convinced that neither death, nor life, nor angels, nor principalities, nor present things, nor future things, nor height, nor depth, nor any other creature will be able to separate us from the love of God." Nothing will separate us from the love of God, from the continuous and persistent call of God. Nothing.

There is no mistake, no transgression, no shortcoming that can keep us from the love of God. God's love for us is unconditional and unending. Sometimes it is our setbacks that put us in touch with this reality in a very poignant way, like they did in the story of the prodigal son. It is our shortcomings that often remind us of our great dependence on God. We need God and God's love desperately, a truth we often forget when we try to control so much: our financial situation, our health, our career path, our use of time, our appearance. We all have some variable, some value, some great need, that we allow to control our lives, instead of handing our decisions over to our Creator.

Though we may feel that we "have it all together," our mistakes serve as a continuous reminder of our utter dependence on God throughout our vocational journey. Our shortcomings are reminders that we do not go about life's journey alone. Our Creator is holding us up, supporting us, sustaining us, and guiding us along the way, no matter how many times we fall. In matters of vocation, we are not in charge. God guides us and loves us because of and despite our shortcomings. St. Paul's wise words remind us that even our mistakes and failures cannot keep us from the all-encompassing love of God.

Our obstacles remind us to "let God be God." They remind us that we are the "created," the creatures, and God is the Creator. God as our Creator is still in charge, and it is good to be reminded of our place and God's place from time to time. Our obstacles do this for us. They remind us of our proper place in our relationship with God. They remind us that we are not God, an important realization for those who take the idea of vocation seriously. It is always God who leads. Let me be me. Let God be God. In the cultivation of and discovery of our vocation, it is God who is in charge.

Our mistakes and failures, by reminding us of our utter dependence on God, call us to humility. The word "humility" comes from the root word *humus,* which means "earth," or "dirt." The word's origin reminds us that we were created from the earth, that we were created from dust. We have humble beginnings.

Humility is not favored in our culture. All one has to do to see this concretely is to look at the self-help section in any major bookstore. Have you ever seen a self-help or lifestyle title that has anything to do with humility? The titles are all about self-sufficiency: *Get the Life You Want, The Seven Habits of Successful People, Ensuring Your Personal Financial Success.* There are no indications that improving one's character might have something to do with the practice of humility. In our culture we often equate humility with meek, self-effacing behavior and other behaviors we view as negative. Humility does not fit neatly into a culture that values being in charge and controlling your own destiny, your own self-improvement.

To be humble does not require us to be self-effacing or self-chastising, however. To be truly humble does not even preclude taking pride in our achievements. There is nothing wrong with celebrating and being excited about the things we do well. That kind of pride, good pride, does not preclude humility.

To be humble is to be continually open to conversion, to new ways of life. To be humble requires that we recognize that the discovery of our vocation is not a moment. It is a process. Humility means we never "arrive." Humility means we are always "arriving." To be humble is to acknowledge that one spends a lifetime in the discovery of a vocation. To be humble is to recognize that we can always, always change for the better. We can always improve who we are. We can always be more true to the person that God is calling us to be. God, through our vocations, invites us to a lifetime of conversion.

Humility is, at its most basic level, two things, according to spiritual writer Joan Chittister. First, it is the ability to deal with life's humiliations in emotionally and spiritually healthy ways. Second, humility is the glue of our relationships and the foundation of community, family, and friendship. Humility has both personal and communal ramifications. It is simply a willingness to be open to God and to others. It does not require us to self-flagellate, to self-doubt. It simply requires of us a radical openness, openness to others and openness to God.

The presence or absence of humility within our persona has major ramifications for how we deal with others. If we expect ourselves to be perfect, or think of ourselves as perfect, we will have that same unreasonable expectation of others. If we are overly impatient with our own shortcomings, then we will have very little patience for the shortcomings of others. We owe it to others to be humble just as much as we owe it to ourselves. Whether or not we are humble has important ramifications for the quality of our interactions with our friends, family, colleagues, and acquaintances. Humility is a practice that opens us both to conversion and to community.

Reject the Rejection

Our obstacles and rejections give rise to some very good things: they teach us humility, they open our hearts to others, they open our souls to God, they force us to utilize creativity and pursue alternative vocational paths. Sometimes it is necessary, however, in the face of great conviction and passion, not to accept a rejection. Sometimes we may feel so strongly and so convicted about an issue or a decision that our hearts do not allow us to take no for an answer. This is especially true in matters of vocation, which are so intimately tied to our passions and convictions. On our vocational journey, it sometimes becomes necessary to reject the rejection. Our resistance to rejection is fueled by passion and by our belief in God's will for us.

One well-known individual in our recent American Catholic history who rejected many rejections was Dorothy Day. Dorothy Day is credited, along with itinerant French philosopher Peter Maurin, with founding the Catholic Worker movement, launched during the Depression and dedicated to following the radical call of the Gospels: clothing the naked, sheltering the homeless, caring for the sick, and burying the dead. The movement that Dorothy Day galvanized went beyond the works of mercy to include acts of direct service as well as acts of political advocacy and social action.

Day was a staunch pacifist and was often arrested for speaking out against the Second World War and the world's buildup of nuclear arsenals. Day was also an excellent writer and used her talents in this way to follow her passion for justice. In the words of writer Robert Ellsberg, "Her vocations as a writer and a radical found their place within a larger vocation. That calling . . . 'means to live in such a way that one's life would not make sense if God did not exist.' "

The Catholic Worker movement began with a penny-a-copy newspaper that echoed the radical call of the Gospels. Many of Day's fifteen hundred articles, essays, and reviews were published in this newspaper. Those who wrote for the newspaper eventually decided that they wanted to practice the hospitality that they wrote of and began to open up Catholic Worker houses to the poor, houses that provided food and shelter to the needy. Over 150 Catholic Worker hospitality houses still exist today, and the Catholic Worker newspaper still has a circulation of a hundred thousand. Its price has now risen to a hefty twenty-five cents per copy.

The Catholic Worker movement is still alive and well, but in its fledgling days it was often treated as an ill-advised embarrassment to the institutional, hierarchical Catholic Church. Dorothy Day and her followers were continually rejected by those who did not share their political and economic beliefs, including members of the Catholic hierarchy. Many Catholics rejected Day because they felt that the church should "stay in church," that is, that the church should attend to spiritual matters only, rather than the white-hot fiery matters of politics and justice. Day was rejected by her "radical" bohemian friends for her decision to convert to Catholicism. She chose, however, day after day, to reject the rejections even of those she had been close to previously. She rejected the rejections of the hierarchy of the church that she loved so much. She rejected the rejections of her fellow Catholics.

Within five years of Dorothy Day's death in 1980, however, the American Catholic bishops published a pastoral on peace, condemning the arms race and allowing for conscientious objection. Popular writers and numerous Catholics had begun to talk about Roman Catholicism as a "peace church," and war resistance had become a very Catholic thing. Many Catholics accepted this idea of the church working for justice long after Dorothy did.

Dorothy Day was a pacifist before it was socially acceptable to be a pacifist. Dorothy Day worked for peace before she was backed by official-sounding church documents. Dorothy Day had stood firm and eventually the church had come around. Fueled by her passions, she found the strength to reject the many rejections and angry missives that were directed her way.

Our newspapers and magazines chronicle stories of the many people who reject rejections and fight obstacles every day. Parents, fueled by a staunch belief in their child's human dignity, fight for adequate health insurance coverage for the health care required by a child's illness. Athletes like Tour de France winner Lance Armstrong fight debilitating diseases with the strong will to live and a deep desire to use their God-given talents. Social workers, teachers, and case managers reject the sentiments of people who tell them, "You could be doing so much more with your education," or "You could be making so much more money." These dedicated individuals are strengthened and sustained by the conviction that they, in the work they chose, fulfill a need in the world and answer a call from God. They reject the rejections, and do so with conviction and great passion.

It is interesting that, though we continue to face rejections and failure throughout our lives, it doesn't seem to get any easier to face them. Each failure gives rise to disappointment that is fresh and new. But somehow we grow beyond each obstacle, a testament to the resilience of the human spirit. If we keep our failures in the right perspective, we recognize them as calls to conversion and community. We recognize them as invitations to exercise creativity. We acknowledge that our failures have a flip side. We acknowledge them as opportunities to journey on holy roads that are less traveled. We remember that in the gradual process of the discovery of our vocation, our failures are just as important as our successes. Often our failures open up doors to sentiments and experiences that our successes cannot.

❧ *Four* ❧

Living in the Sun and the Shade

When we celebrate a wedding, we celebrate a union as well as a departure. When we celebrate death we celebrate lost friendship as well as gained liberty. There can be tears after weddings and smiles after funerals. Life and death are not opponents but do, in fact, kiss each other at every moment of our existence.

—Henri Nouwen, *Creative Ministry*

I never understood people who lost their faith in the face of tragedy. I would hear and read personal accounts of people, who, in the face of tragedy, would "lose it," turning to alcohol or drugs. Their stories — chronicled in the pages of *People* magazine, thick autobiographical tomes, or a segment on *Oprah* — often described personal doubts of the existence of God and a turn away from organized religion following the tragic death of a friend or the debilitating illness of a family member.

Many people who have endured extreme tragedy refer to a stage of complete loss of hope and faith. I never used to be able to understand why they turned away from God — even for just a little while — at a time when they needed their faith the most. Their descriptions of downward spirals of emotion and anger toward God never made sense to me — until Gretchen got sick, really sick.

Gretchen, my thirteen-year-old sister, was diagnosed with cancer when I was a senior in high school. The devastating diagnosis was a complete surprise. For the previous few weeks she had not been feeling well, had been sleeping a lot, and had undergone a variety of medical tests to determine what the problem was. Most medical professionals seemed to think her lack of energy was the result of some sort of thyroid gland problem. To be honest, I do not even remember worrying much when she underwent her medical tests. I just assumed that her diagnosis would be a fixable affliction that could be cured by an over-the-counter drug or some extra sleep.

When the test results arrived at the hospital lab, the news shocked us all. Incurable cancer. The memory of the September day when we received the test results is imprinted indelibly on my mind and soul. I was a high-energy, fairly focused senior in high school at the time, and my thoughts in those days rarely strayed from my sky-is-the-limit-and-anything-is-possible mentality. The flow of sunshine and optimism came to an abrupt halt when I returned home from cross-country practice one day and my parents pulled me out into the front yard to tell me about the test results. Cancer.

Words cannot describe the shock, horror, and fear that I felt upon hearing the news that my sister was going to die. I couldn't fathom losing my only sister—my beautiful, feisty, smart, in-love-with-life sister. I could not imagine life without her. I couldn't imagine how she could be so sick. Bad things like this weren't supposed to happen to people in my family. We were normal. We had things to do, places to go. Debilitating sickness was not part of our plan.

Eventually, the shock gave way to anger. Intense anger. I had a few choice words for the God whom I had (mistakenly?) thought to be so loving and protective, the God whom I thought would be able to help me accomplish anything I set my mind to. Who was this God who would allow my sister to undergo such lengthy, intense physical and mental suffering? Certainly not the God I thought I knew.

With Gretchen's bad news in the forefront of my mind, my inner spiritual interrogation began. I questioned why God would permit my parents to endure the pain of losing a child. I grew angry not only with God but with those around me whose lives seemed so normal and flawless. I remember watching groups of kids ride their bikes in our neighborhood and questioning why everyone in their families appeared to be in perfect health. Why did everyone around me seem to have such carefree, perfect lives? Why did "everyone else" get to have a sister, or many sisters, and soon, though I did not even know how soon, I would be forced to part with mine against my will?

At the age of sixteen I had heard many times, from multiple sources, that life was not fair, but never did those sources tell me that when I personally discovered life was not fair, that realization would cause my heart to feel like it was being stepped on by someone wearing steel-toe boots and to feel like my insides were being pulled out of me, leaving me hollow and empty. All of a sudden, I very clearly understood how easy it was to lose one's faith in the face of devastating news, especially when the news concerns someone you love deeply and cannot imagine living without. All of a sudden, I comprehended why many strong people grow weak in the face of doubt, despair, and uncertainty.

Gretchen battled cancer heroically for a year and a half. I continue to stand in awe of the courage she showed at the age of thirteen. Despite the hair loss, fatigue, and sickness that the chemotherapy caused her, she continued to pursue the activities that she had always loved: ballet, skiing, and playing with her best friends Marta and Kerry. She maintained a steady presence in her ballet classes and faithfully showed up at her dance school whenever she was feeling good enough.

She attended enough ballet classes that she was able to both learn and perform the dance for the spring recital. She had completely lost her hair at that point. Her baldness, however, did not deter her from performing in front of hundreds of people that night. Among the other petite thirteen-year-old ballerinas, their hair pulled back into tight buns, her smooth, bare head was yet another testament to the dare-to-be different attitude for which she was so well known throughout her life. I will always remember how graceful and pretty she was on the night of her ballet recital. Her young face, pierced with bright blue eyes, expressed a mixture of determination, self-confidence, and peace.

Gretchen's display of courage and resolve on that spring evening will always serve as an inspiring memory for me. It is a memory that, in my most difficult moments, enables me to act with courage. When I find myself in adverse situations, I will always remember how, even in the face of debilitating cancer treatments, Gretchen continued to dance. She was a symbol of all that is good and beautiful that is always with us, despite appearances.

On the days when Gretchen wasn't feeling well, her best friends, Marta and Kerry, kept a vigil by her side on our family room couch. They watched her favorite movies with her, brought her favorite foods, and tried to make her laugh by telling her funny stories. My parents, both in the medical field, cared for her around the clock until the day she died, a cold February day when her pain and suffering finally came to an end. I was away at college when the dreaded phone call came. Though it was extremely painful to hear that Gretchen had died, I felt immediate relief that she no longer had to suffer. I knew that Gretchen was in heaven, where she was probably dancing, finally free from the afflictions and debilitating effects of cancer.

After the initial relief subsided, I began the long process of grieving the loss of my little sister. During this difficult time, though I suffered, I felt that I was not alone. My faith was strengthened by the outpouring of compassion and support that our family received both during and after Gretchen's funeral. I really felt that God was present through our friends and family during those dark, lonely days, although I do not know exactly how I knew it was God. I just did.

She Lives in You

God came to us in the form of generous, loving, and faith-filled people who shared with us what Gretchen's life had meant to them. God came to us in the people who delivered lasagna and sandwiches and sent cards and flowers. God came to us in the angelic voices of the thirty students from my college choir who drove seventy-five miles to sing and play instruments for Gretchen's funeral. Even in the darkest of those February days, I knew that I was not alone. I somehow knew that God was with me.

These thoughtful people did not take away my pain, but in the face of death their presence helped me to feel something *other* than pain, at least for short periods of time. The generosity of friends, family, and neighbors has taught me how to reach out to other people now when their loved ones die — something I never knew how to do before. Their example was a very poignant lesson in the practice of the virtue of compassion. The lasting effects of their kind gestures remind me of a phrase from Joan Chittister, who defines compassion in the following way: "Compassion is the first funeral you attend after one of your loved ones dies." How true I find those words to be now.

I do feel now that I am a more compassionate person because of the way I was ministered to after Gretchen's death. I have realized that to practice compassion is an instrumental part of living one's vocation. We all will be called to practice compassion in a variety of situations. Though I do not embody compassion perfectly or constantly, I have grasped what it means to practice compassion and better understand its importance.

Gretchen's death also reminded me, in a very poignant way, of the importance of the corporal works of mercy. At one time the works of mercy were just words on a page to me, nice, humanistic ideas captured neatly in a religion textbook list. I had once memorized the works of mercy in grade school: feed the hungry, give drink to the thirsty, clothe the naked, visit the imprisoned, shelter the homeless, visit the sick, and bury the dead. I could have recited this list to anyone from memory, but never really knew, when I quoted the simple phrase "Bury the dead," what that meant in terms of real-life practices. To bury the dead, I thought, was the responsibility solely of the stiff and somber dark-suited men who worked in funeral homes.

Now I realize that it is the Christian community who buries the dead. Burying the dead is not left to those who work in the funeral business. Because of the compassion that was shown to my family and me in the face of death, I now know what it means to help others bury the dead. I know how very important the simple gift of presence is at a wake or a funeral. To bury the dead means to send a note to someone who has lost a friend or family member, even if you do not know that person well, even if you have never met the person who has died. To bury the dead means to remember and acknowledge the one-year, five-year, or ten-year anniversary of a death, because families and friends do not forget. To bury the dead is to share little stories and anecdotes about the person who has died. To bury the dead is to practice compassion, to be a light for those who are living in darkness. We are all called to bury the dead and to practice the other works of mercy as well.

In those dark days after Gretchen's funeral, I felt that God came to me in the form of a mission—a responsibility I had to carry out after Gretchen died. The day I discovered this mission was on the night that I returned to school after Gretchen's death. Back in my dorm room at Notre Dame, posted on the wall over my desk, was a beautiful collage that my very artistic friend Seana had created for me while I was gone. The collage was a kaleidoscope of colored paper scraps that encircled the simple sentence:

She lives in you.

Tears sprung to my eyes as I read those simple, powerful words, and realized that yes, Gretchen did live on in me. I felt both very weak and very strong as I gazed at those words and set down the luggage I had carried into my room. It was up to me to carry Gretchen's memory with me, to tell other people her story and to live all that was good in her: her smile, her feistiness, her courage, her tremendous spirit, her love of life. That day, keeping Gretchen's memory alive and living all that was good in her became an integral part of my vocation. Emulating her courage and her love of life became something to strive for on my vocational journey.

In reading the words that Seana had written, I also began to better grasp what it means, as a Christian, to believe in resurrection. As I reflected on the words "She lives in you," I thought to myself, "Well maybe this is what resurrection means, in part at least." Maybe resurrection means that, when a person dies, that person lives on in those they have touched. They live on in the stories and the example they pass on.

Resurrection, I believe, means that we carry with us the living presence of those who have died. Resurrection also means that we can pray to the people who have gone before us. I used to pray *for* Gretchen when she was so sick and weak. Now I can pray *to* her, listen *to* her, and ask for her protection and help. I have a special friend in heaven that I can ask to pray for me and for those in need. Though Gretchen is gone, I sense that she still will communicate with me, although in different ways than I am accustomed to. She communicates with me through her spirit. I continually call upon her in all kinds of situations, both the triumphant and the trying.

I have found comfort when I have discovered, many times, that I am not the only one who engages in this kind of prayerful communication. In her autobiography, *The Virgin of Bennington,* poet and spiritual writer Kathleen Norris writes of the experience of losing a dear companion and mentor. A monk friend said to Norris after her mentor's death: "Just because your friend is gone doesn't mean you have to stop listening to her," and Norris takes in this advice. She writes:

> I do listen to Betty, in many ways. When I tend my thriving patch of sorrel, parsley, and tarragon, I wonder if by observing her in Rhode Island, I learned gardening by osmosis. I feel her presence whenever I add a pinch of nutmeg to cooked spinach, as it is a trick she taught me.

I have found this monk's simple advice, a simple exhortation to listen, to be quite helpful. I can still communicate with my sister, Gretchen. She can still guide and be present to me as I continue to journey through life. There have been many, many times when I have recognized my need for her help.

When Gretchen was alive she used to help me repeatedly with two practices: finding my geographical direction and locating lost possessions. She was both my compass and my own personal St. Anthony-on-earth. God has given me many talents, but I have not been blessed with a good sense of direction or a large capacity for short-term memory. As a result, I often get lost while I am driving and constantly misplace my possessions.

I am convinced that it is Gretchen who has helped me find my way on back country roads at night and helped me to navigate unfamiliar interstates when I travel. I am convinced that it is Gretchen who has helped me locate wallets, insurance cards, important receipts, and various pieces of jewelry that seem to have sprouted legs and run at the most inconvenient times. Though I still miss her terribly, I do find some comfort in the idea that I have some sort of "special protector and seeker" in heaven.

My family and I continue to keep Gretchen's memory alive by retelling stories about her whenever she comes to mind. We usually call one another on both her birthday and the anniversary of her death, just to check in and share our support. These anniversaries are always a struggle. I've tried all kinds of ways of commemorating them, including trying to ignore the dates, which has never been very effective. But some means of commemorating Gretchen's anniversaries have been very powerful.

One year, when my brother and I were living on the same college campus, we decided to have a Mass said in her honor. He and I were entrusted with the preaching task that day, and so after the Gospel was read we both shared our thoughts on what her life had meant to us. As I prepared my reflections I was struck by the fact that none of the people who would be attending the Mass had ever known Gretchen. They were all people that Justin and I had met a few years after her death. Again, that sense of mission bubbled to the surface of my consciousness. I felt a real need to fully convey to people what kind of person Gretchen was and what qualities she demonstrated. I felt the need to share some of her stories.

These are the words I spoke to our small congregation that day. I hope they conveyed to our friends that they actually knew Gretchen better than they may have thought they did:

If, when you go to the beach, you are always the last person to get out of the water, then you know Gretchen.

If you have ever shown courage, then you know Gretchen.

If you give your brothers and sisters a hard time, then you know Gretchen.

If you like to collect stones and rocks from the beach, then you know Gretchen.

If you know Justin and me, then you know Gretchen.

If you like to dance, then you know Gretchen.

> If you try to squeeze as much out of life as you can, then you
>   know Gretchen.

I felt as if I did live up to my mission that day by sharing these words, and this sense was later confirmed by a friend of mine who said to me, "Now I feel like I'm getting to know Gretchen better all the time."

Though telling Gretchen's story does not always serve to lessen my grief, it certainly helps me to better feel her presence. In Barbara Kingsolver's novel *Animal Dreams,* the protagonist, Codi, describes her own grief process as she comes to grips with the sudden death of her sister Hallie, who was killed while working as a political activist in Nicaragua.

> I finished by reading the letter from Sister Sabina Martin. She said thousands of people joined us in mourning Hallie. "I know that it doesn't make your grief any smaller," she wrote, "but I believe it makes Hallie's presence larger. Certainly, she won't be forgotten."

When we tell the stories of those who have gone to God before us, those who most of the time have left us much, much too soon, we feel their presence more acutely when we share their stories with others. It does not make our grief smaller, but it does make their presence larger.

Light and Darkness

The time leading up to and immediately following Gretchen's death was the darkest time I have experienced to this date. "You'll be made of steel after going through this," said my dad. "This may be the worst thing you ever endure." I hope he is right, but I realize that this may not be the case. There is surely more darkness ahead, more challenges and difficulties, though I do not know what form they will take. But I do not face the darkness with quite as much trepidation as I did before, for the simple reason that I was shown light in the darkness of Gretchen's death. In our vocational journeys, no matter how overwhelming the darkness seems to be, we can always find small points of light.

Even in the midst of the darkness and pain of Gretchen's death, I saw light and hope from time to time, proof positive of the words of the Gospel of John that "the light shines in the darkness, and the darkness does not overcome it." The points of light were the college friendships that were strengthened by my friends' sharing in my suffering, the close relationship with my brother that he and I now share, and my heightened awareness of other people's grief and suffering. In the whole experience of Gretchen's suffering and death, light and darkness existed together. Death and life, light and darkness came hand in hand, or, in the words of Henri Nouwen, "kissed each other at every moment."

If we believe in the Christian story, the paschal mystery, that is, the life, death, and resurrection of Jesus, then we believe that life and death, joy and sorrow, light and darkness, day and night, will always go hand in hand. These opposing forces do not cancel each other out; they exist together and form a complete cycle. They always will. To truly live out a Christian vocation is to acknowledge this truth.

To live the paschal mystery is to believe that there will be light in the darkness, that the shadows of darkness may sometimes dim the light, that there will be hope in the midst of the sorrow, that there will be struggles even in the face of great joy. To believe in the paschal mystery is to acknowledge that light and darkness exist side by side, that the line between the sun and the shade is very, very thin. One step is all it takes to leave the cool comfort of a shady glen and enter the bright, hot light of the blazing sun. One step is all it takes to emerge from a dark room into the guiding and inspiring light of day.

To be aware of the paschal mystery is to acknowledge that death is only a cancer diagnosis or a car accident away. To live the paschal mystery is to acknowledge that the cross, the instrument of Christ's death, is there, stark and foreboding, but that it is not the end of the story. Hope, light, and resurrection exist on the other side of death and darkness. To embrace a vocation requires us to embrace this reality, this guiding sequence in our lives.

Most of the time, the dyings and risings, the losses and gains that we undergo, large and small, are forced upon us against our will. But other times we make vocational decisions and commitments that galvanize this cycle of loss and gain, joy and sadness, life and death. This cycle is guaranteed to repeat itself many times as life happens to us and as we make vocational choices. To embrace our vocation, that is, the life that God calls us to live, is to embrace both the light and the darkness that it entails. The choices we make will often close as many doors as they open.

Vocation is just as much about how we react to the cards that have been dealt to us as it is about the commitments we make. We invite the paschal mystery into our lives by our decisions. By saying yes to one thing we have to say no to another. By saying yes to marriage we give up some of our independence. By saying yes to an upward move within a corporation we say goodbye to some of our free time and naiveté. By saying yes to a simple lifestyle we part with some comforts, conveniences, and status symbols. By saying no to temptation in a difficult situation we feel the satisfaction and deep peace that come from doing the right thing. In our attempt to live the life that God calls us to live, we inevitably live the paschal mystery, in small ways, over and over again. Dying and rising, joy and sorrow, light and darkness always come into our lives hand in hand. As we spend a lifetime discerning our vocation, we will continually invite this cycle into our lives by the decisions we make.

If there is a single lesson that Gretchen's death taught me, it is that even when darkness is present in our lives, by chance, by fate, or as a result of a decision we make, the light will always prevail. Never has that been clearer than on the night of Gretchen's ballet recital. Her example continues to be a source of hope to me. As I enter my late twenties the decisions I make seem to have more and more at stake. Issues and variables to weigh seem to become more and more complicated. I know that by choosing to live in a certain city, deciding on a person to date, pursuing future education in a particular area of study, practicing my faith in a certain way I am closing certain doors to myself, some of them permanently. Thinking about those closed doors can be quite overwhelming. But, at the same time, I always try to remember the beautiful words from Scripture, that "the one who loses a life will find it," or "Knock, and the door will be opened to you." Sometimes we have to lose our lives, in a sense, to find them. Sometimes we must shed some of who we are to become who God is calling us to be. To fruitfully discover our vocation requires us to cast off some of our old comfortable lifestyles and habits, to trust in the God who says, "Behold, I make all things new."

Our Mornings...

We see the cycle of death and new life, darkness and light, in the simple rhythm of our days. The basic cosmic cycle that shapes and guides our regular activities, the cycle of morning to evening, of day to night and back to day, mirrors the cycle of death and resurrection that we live. The cycle of a twenty-four-hour period dictates our sleeping and our waking, our work and our leisure, our "gearing up" and our relaxing. Many of us refer to being either "a night person" or "a morning person." I have been both, at different points in my life, as circumstance has dictated and demanded. I have come to love qualities of both morning and evening, both day and night. And I would not be able to appreciate one without the other. Day would not encapsulate such hope and promise if it were not preceded by darkness, and night would not deliver such mystery and uncertainty without the sensual stimulation of the day.

Living out our vocation has everything to do with the decisions we make in the mornings and the evenings of our lives, both literally and figuratively. To listen to God's call is to acknowledge the newness, the potential, the freshness, and the gift of light that morning presents. To listen to God's call is to recognize in our evenings the quiet of darkness, the opportunity for rest and reflection, the confrontation of truths that the day's distractions do not allow. Sometimes our lives will be filled with the stuff of mornings: time, opportunity, energy, promise, big plans,

and light to illuminate our path. At other times our lives will be replete with the stuff of night: darkness, blindness, rest, fear, strange
sounds whose source we cannot see. The cycle of darkness and
light is an indispensable guiding force in our gradual discovery of
vocation.

The interplay of morning and evening is the cycle that guides
our living and being. It is all that we as limited human beings have
to work with. We discover and live out our vocation within this
simple, sometimes predictable and repetitive, sequence of morning and evening, light and darkness. It is the little choices we make,
day in and day out, the tiniest decisions that form our habits and
our routines, that often determine our vocational paths just as
much as the bigger decisions do. How we deal with the "stuff"
of regular days, the constant cycle of morning and evening, has
everything to do with what kind of person we become and what
we contribute to the world.

I have always wanted to be a morning person. Yet somehow
the idea of waking up early hasn't quite taken root in me. "I love
mornings," I used to tell people, "but I just have trouble with that
whole transition between night and day." As I have gotten a bit
older I have appreciated more and more the unique opportunities
that morning offers. For example, I've grown to cherish a morning
run, a run that, if it begins early enough, is free of noise and the
dodging of traffic, free from the intense, burning heat of the sun.
When I run in the morning I am rejuvenated and can begin my
workday with at least a small sense of accomplishment. It is gratifying to arrive at the office knowing that I've already completed a
small task, and an enjoyable and energizing one at that. I feel that
I can better help others and have a more positive attitude when I
have begun my day in a healthy way.

In addition to running, there is another morning ritual that has
made its claim on me. I've developed a fierce, almost romantic, at-
tachment to sipping a mug of hot coffee while reading the morning
paper. There is something calming (and delightfully stimulating,
if you drink caffeinated coffee) about beginning each day with
the same familiar concoction, an unchanging combination of coffee, milk, and sugar, maybe even sipped from the same cup or

travel mug every time. I've grown to appreciate the whole coffee-and-newspaper experience: the inevitable caffeine jump-start, the morning's news headlines, the pontification of pundits in the op-ed pages, the sports scores, the local section that features the sometimes charming "hometown kid does good" stories.

It is good, as we begin our day, to familiarize ourselves with the challenges, triumphs, tragedies, issues, and concerns that are chronicled in the news. With the morning paper we begin our day with an awareness of our place in the world and a better sense of what is required of us. Maybe we read stories of world hunger and are moved, and are subsequently chastened by our own abundance and privilege. Maybe we peruse the opinion pages in order to make an informed voting decision. Maybe we scan the entertainment section to see what is on television tonight and decide how we are going to allot our free time. We may examine the obituaries looking for familiar names. An activity as simple as reading the morning paper can shape how we conduct ourselves throughout the day. It is an activity that provides perspective. Reflecting on the news, however briefly, can help us to identify needs and get a better sense of our place in the world.

A glance at the morning newspaper can even shape how we pray. It is just as important, vocationally, to "pray the news" as it is to pray for our own personal concerns, cares, and worries. Good, solid prayer draws us outward just as much as it draws us inward. Prayer that is truly wholistic moves us to eventual action. I was introduced to this idea of praying the news, not by an article in the newspaper, but, ironically, from a website maintained by the contemplative Carmelite sisters of Indianapolis. The website (*http://praythenews.com*) is aptly named *Pray the News* and posts a news clip each week that is accompanied by the contemplative reflections of seven Carmelite sisters. Why pray the news at all? The sisters' explanation is quite thought-provoking:

> All too often, it seems, there is no one to free the oppressed, uphold the fallen, or shelter the homeless. We may view these events through a television screen, the front page of a newspaper — or even the eyes of someone who has seen.

However they come to us, these painful reminders of the incompleteness of the world are everywhere.

It is in this context, then, that we pray the news. By continuously making ourselves aware of the present moment of the universe, we awaken ourselves to our presence to God — and in our own way, participate in the healing, loving and creative energy this process can spark.

It is by praying the news that we are awakened to both God's presence and to the needs of the world around us. Praying the news provides a morning "wake-up call": it provides an awareness of the presence of God, an attentiveness to the needy, a call to action, a call to help heal the incompleteness of the world. Even a morning ritual of coffee and a newspaper, seemingly simple, ostensibly routine, can shape who we are, can contour our contributions to the world. Mornings provide us with the gift of a daily fresh start, a new chance to be the person God is calling us to be. Praying the news can be an important part of one's vocation. The practice itself is representative of the fact that all of our vocations call us outward to transform the places of need in our world.

By praying the news in the morning or beginning our day with some form of reflection, we imitate the practice of our Christian ancestors, who have from the beginning marked the morning and the evening with prayer. Even the psalms of the official morning prayer of the church speak of both the great need and the bountiful blessings that grace our world each day. "The Lord keeps faith for ever," says Psalm 146, "giving food to the hungry, justice to the poor, freedom to captives. The Lord opens blind eyes and straightens the bent, comforting widows and the orphans, protecting the stranger." "Sun and moon, glittering stars, sing praise, sing praise," says Psalm 148. "Fire and hail, snow and mist, storms, winds, mountains, hills, fruit trees and cedars, wild beasts and tame, snakes and birds, princes, judges, rulers, subjects, men, women, old and young, praise, praise the holy name beyond all names." Thus, even the ancient morning psalms of the church recognize that the morning brings with it both the praiseworthy and the petition-worthy. Morning is a sacred time.

. . . *and Our Evenings*

Evenings are just as rife with opportunity for reflection. The night, characterized by quiet, uncertainty, and darkness, provides its own panoply of opportunities, its own sacred rituals. Night is a time of supper, a time of rest, a time of catching up on chores, a time for making phone calls. It is a time to reflect on what has happened during our day, to anticipate, with fear, excitement, or dread, what will happen tomorrow. It is a time when we confront concerns from which the day has distracted us. Night is sacred, holy time.

For some reason, perhaps because of the darkness and quiet, worries, concerns, and fears seem to be more formidable at night. Nighttime does not, for the most part, provide the stimulation and whirlwind of activity that the daytime does, and this freedom of distraction forces us to confront the issues and concerns we were able to shelve during the day while we were busy with other pursuits. Darkness hides most visible things, forcing us to rely on experiences of sound, touch, and intuition. Darkness, both literally and figuratively, calls us to trust.

But darkness seems to encourage our worries to come out of hiding. Sunday nights often seem particularly overwhelming. A couple of years ago an article in *Newsweek* reported that, according to sleep experts, Sunday nights were the time, above all other times, when people encountered the most difficulty sleeping. On Sunday nights a week of responsibilities and requirements looms, and our to-do lists are at their longest. When worry and stress creep into my mind in the evenings I try to recall the simple advice my mom gave me long ago: "It won't seem so bad in the morning. Everything seems worse at night." I have found that she is right. I also have found that her advice to say some silent Hail Marys, instead of the oft-recommended counting sheep, has been a helpful practice. I was very skeptical when my mom first recommended this practice, but now it is second nature, and the monotony of a memorized prayer provides another distraction from worry until the day comes. Lately, I've also found comfort in the Canticle of Simeon, an integral part of the church's night prayer. It is another

good phrase to commit to memory and to pray as our day draws
to a close:

> Protect us, Lord, as we stay awake;
> Watch over us as we sleep,
> That, awake, we may keep watch with Christ,
> And, asleep, rest in Christ's peace.

Though problems and worries do not vanish with the night prayers
or the coming of dawn, the morning light does bring new energy
and new perspective to deal with these cares.

I also have found that, when we are confronted by darkness, it
is helpful to choose carefully what we read before we fall asleep.
Keep some books by your bed that are uplifting or reflective, and
this may help to calm your thoughts before you drift off to sleep.
Some of the most restless nights I ever had were when my nighttime reading was *The Things They Carried,* by Tim O'Brien. This
Pulitzer prizewinner about the Vietnam War was certainly worth-
while reading, but vivid scenes of booby-trapped tropical jungles,
bloody wartime atrocities, and violent nightmarish stories did not
for a good night's sleep make and did little to temporarily alleviate
my worries. Since then I have been more careful about my evening
reading choices. The writings of Barbara Kingsolver, Anne Lamott,
Joan Chittister, Andre Dubus, and Henri Nouwen have proven to
be more appropriate literary choices for the later hours of the day.

Night may bring our worries into sharper relief, but it also provides us with the gift of a completed day. The end of a day, with
its memories of deeds, conversations, and decisions, provides rich
material for evening reflection, however brief it is. Night provides
a time to look within ourselves and say, "Okay God, how did I do
today?" A more official-sounding, more intentional way of looking
at this question is to take a few minutes in the evening, maybe the
few minutes before we drift off to sleep, to do a brief examination
of conscience. This can serve as a reminder of the vocation we all
have, to strive with all our being to reach our God-given potential in our work, our leisure, our service, and our daily interactions
with others.

The examination, or examen, of conscience is an ancient practice of the church. Jesuit scripture scholar Dennis Hamm refers to it as "rummaging for God" or "praying backward through your day." St. Ignatius included the examen as one of the practices in his *Spiritual Exercises.* To do an examen, to "pray backward through your day" is to acknowledge that God has been present to us throughout the day. We rummage through the clutter of our day in the hope of uncovering both our blessings and our shortcomings, and possibly to discover some semblance of how God may be leading us.

There are many ways of practicing the examen, but in its most basic form it involves three steps: to review the day in thanksgiving, to review the feelings that surface in the "reliving" of the day, and to look toward the needs and opportunities of tomorrow. In a nutshell, we ask ourselves two questions: What am I grateful for? What am I not grateful for?

By reviewing the day in thanksgiving and gratitude we acknowledge the God-given gifts of health, of work, of relationships, or other gifts that have graced our day. By reviewing the feelings that surfaced during the day we are better able to determine which emotions guided our actions. Were we motivated today by jealousy? generosity? selfishness? patience or impatience? In looking to tomorrow's events — the happenings that fill our planners and palm pilots — we ask God for help, healing, confidence, or humility, for guidance during another day. We end the examen with the Lord's Prayer, the simple prayer many of us have known since childhood.

To end our day with this brief examen is to acknowledge that God continues to work within our day-to-day experiences, however mundane they seem, and continues to love us, faults and all, however manifold our shortcomings may be. If we are faithful to the habit of reflecting on what we are both grateful and not grateful for, we will gradually come to a greater familiarity with what gives us life, which will help our decision-making tremendously.

Our nights and mornings, joys and sorrows, dyings and risings are the raw materials we use to build the lives God calls us to live. The paschal mystery, the life, death, and resurrection of Jesus, is the cycle that encircles and permeates our vocation. To live out our vocations is to embrace this sequence, to jump right in, with the confidence that our story always ends in hope, that God often draws straight with crooked lines, that God is present to us both in the sun and the shade. To live out a vocation is to acknowledge that our story always ends, as Jesus' did, with both the promise and reality of resurrection and new life. Little did I know that the person to teach me this lesson most profoundly and indelibly would be a feisty, mischievous, brave little thirteen-year-old, who danced when no one thought she could.

❧ *Five* ❧

Living to Work, Working to Live

Hands to work, hearts to God
— Shaker dictum

I cannot remember exactly when I first discovered the value of money and the necessity of work, but I do have distinct early memories of some pretty profitable lemonade stands. My brother and sister and I would gather a neighborhood crew together, pull the cans of Minute Maid out of the freezer, mix the frozen lemonade cylinders and water using a big wooden spoon, and set up shop right near the curb on our residential street. As we got older, we raised the price of our lemonade, but we always gave free drinks to runners and walkers. Business must have been slow one afternoon, because I remember one or two of us actually standing in the middle of the street to stop moving cars. One man reached out the car window with fifty cents in his hand and said impatiently, "I don't want any lemonade. I just want to get through."

When the lemonade stand days ended I held a variety of jobs as I grew up, thanks to the temporary agency I usually relied on during the summers. I worked as a receptionist in a paper mill, a museum exhibit interpreter, a gofer at the local chamber of commerce, and a grade school science teacher, among assorted other positions. I picked up a few insights from each of these, but it was my part-time job as a waitress during my graduate school years that taught me the most. I worked for two years at a family-owned Italian restaurant, a quaint, romantic venue that was often classified by people as "a good date place."

89

I was trained by a woman named Barb, who had worked there "forever," in her words. Her skin was leathery and dark from too many hours in the tanning booth, her voice thick and raspy from too many cigarettes. Her grammar was terrible and her vocabulary was laced with profanity. Barb and I couldn't have been more different, couldn't have had less in common, but I liked her for some reason. There was a strange sort of wisdom that she had, a worldliness about her that came not from having traveled the world, but from living a hard life and trying to make it as a single mother. I liked her because she took her job seriously and worked very hard.

During my first couple of days on the job she led me around the restaurant in a whirlwind, orchestrating a steady parade of heavy lasagna plates and steaming pasta fagioli soup bowls from the kitchen to the dining rooms. We wrapped piles of silverware in white napkins, and I watched her fingers dance quickly back and forth over the cash register keys. She wrote down the names and phone numbers of stores where I could buy the components of my uniform: white tuxedo shirt, green bowtie and cummerbund, black pants. This harried, hands-on orientation, with an unorthodox but very knowledgeable teacher, was my introduction to the working world of waiting tables.

I think everyone should have a food service job at some point in their lives. Eating out is much more commonplace than it used to be, and so working in a restaurant environment provides an interesting window into the quirks, habits, and diversity of humanity. Waiting tables taught me many things, but first and foremost it taught me humility. Nobody in that restaurant cared that I had aced my midterm or recently written a killer paper that had gotten rave faculty reviews. At Francesco's, what mattered was that you posted your appetizer orders on time (antipasto takes longer than bruschetta, breadsticks are garnished with a sprig of parsley, tomato salads are only served in the summer) and kept customers happy.

I certainly was no natural as a waitress. I had more than my fair share of incidents that kept my ego firmly in check during the two years that I worked at the restaurant. There was the time I dropped (and shattered) a glass jar full of red pepper flakes all over the table of a young couple out on a date. (One of them just happened to be a classmate who looked like he could have been an Armani model.) As he and his date sat covered in red-pepper-flake confetti, he said good naturedly, "Don't worry about it. It just looks like we're having a party back here." And then there was the time I whirled around too quickly with a plate of lasagna, and before I knew it, it was airborne. The lasagna flew off the plate and landed on the kitchen floor with a squishy, juicy thud. It took me days to endear myself to the cooks again after losing their freshly made lasagna during the busiest hours of the night.

It was both the mistakes I made and the hands-on, physical, roll-up-your-sleeves nature of this job that taught me greater humility. I usually drove home at the end of a weekend night with tired legs and a white shirt covered with marinara sauce. To live under the constitution of a restaurant, "The customer is always right," is to swallow one's own opinions and bite one's tongue, even when confronted by crochety clientele. It wasn't always easy to pretend that nothing would please me more than to bring another butter packet to a customer, or to feign delight when I was asked to bring out a round of spumoni (which always took forever to scoop out because the freezer kept it so cold and hard).

Working weekends and nights, when I would have rather spent time with friends or worked on a paper, sharpened my consciousness a bit. It enabled me to be more appreciative of all the people who work weekends, people whom I had previously taken for granted. Since my restaurant experience I have been more appreciative of people like the gas station attendants who fill up my tank in the midst of a late-night drive, retail salespeople who fold the clothes I've tried on and discarded, the pharmacists who work at twenty-four-hour drug stores so I can pick up my medicine in the middle of the night.

On one weekend evening at the restaurant I waited on a group of administrators from the university I was attending. One of them recognized me and said, "Oh, it's great that you are working here. This job is your *diakonia*." I have to admit that at the time I didn't know what she meant. So when I got home that night I looked it up in the dictionary and discovered that *diakonia* is a Greek word meaning "to serve" and the root of the word "deacon."

Looking upon my job as service, *diakonia,* did enrich my whole experience. I thought about how people often come to restaurants to celebrate important occasions: birthdays, anniversaries, business negotiations, job offers. I liked to think of myself as serving so others could celebrate. As members of a working society we all serve. We work to make money of course, but also to serve one another. We serve our local communities and our families. We work to enrich our professions. Lawyers work to ensure that all people receive a fair trial and due process. Construction workers provide safe roadways that allow people to visit their families and take business trips. Physicians restore health and alleviate pain. The economy, the working world, exists to serve humanity, and we as the fledgling members of the work force are a pivotal part of the system.

Holy Work, Good Examples

The very act of work is sacred and holy, though it may not always seem that way when we're caught up in a lunchroom trash-the-boss session or a contentious staff meeting. Work at its best is meaningful and full of purpose. We can look to God, to Jesus, to the saints, and to ordinary people we encounter day-to-day to learn that work can have tremendous meaning. James Martin, a Jesuit priest, in the introduction to the book *Patrons and Protectors,* writes: "Perhaps the most overlooked truth in Christian history is that Jesus worked." Though we don't read much about it in Scripture, Jesus must have spent many hours in the woodshop with his father, Joseph, learning the tricks of the trade and refining his skills as a carpenter. The saints worked too. Though they are often portrayed piously and motionlessly in art, gazing skyward as if in ecstasy, they had day jobs too, and did them well — part of the reason they are now saints. St. Katherine Drexel built schools, churches, and missions around the country. St. Albert the Great loved science and taught in some of the best universities of his day. During the black plague St. Catherine of Siena worked through the night, digging graves for the dead and visiting the sick in their homes.

The fact that Jesus and the saints worked has made the very act of work holy. By taking on our humanity fully Jesus made human qualities holy, including our ability to work. By working hard themselves the saints created examples for us to follow, both in the kind of work they did and the attitudes they cultivated as they carried on with their life's work. They've made some good inroads for us on the path of life. One of my favorite theologians, Elizabeth Johnson, in her book *Friends of God and Prophets,* uses a phrase from St. Augustine that captures the saints' pioneering contributions very well: "By passing along the narrow road they widened it, and while they went along, tramping on the rough ways, they went ahead of us." We stand on the shoulders of the saints. Though they never faced the same kinds of specific hassles that we now face in the workplace (downsizing, frozen computer screens, eighty-hour work weeks), they certainly worked hard, relied on their gifts and talents, and in the meantime found a way to live lives worth emulating.

God worked to create the heavens and earth and the creatures that inhabit them, and this means that our work, our creations, are holy too. This is what it means to be *imago Dei,* to be made in the image and likeness of God. To be *imago Dei* means to have the ability to create in a variety of ways, and our work is one of them. In our jobs, in whatever we may do, we are co-creators with God. There is a creative energy in our work that is connected with God's creative energy. If we can internalize and believe in that connection, that awareness can shape our attitudes and our work. In our work as co-creators we have the best possible supervisor who never takes days off, who takes delight in our labors, who forgives our every flaw.

To acknowledge that work is sacred and holy doesn't mean that you need to think pious thoughts on the subway or to reflect explicitly on your faith as you slog through a long workday. There are just about as many ways to link your faith and your work as there are jobs listed on *Monster.com.* How to make the connection will depend on you, of course, and the kind of work you do.

One way to integrate your faith and your work, in the words of the late Archbishop Oscar Romero, is "to step back every once in a while and take the long view." Just take a few moments to reflect on your day when it is done, maybe right before dinner or in those brief moments before you drift off to sleep. Often our workdays are so crazy and hectic that we lose perspective of what we are doing and whom we are doing it for. Retrospect at the end of the day can be a real gift and can help uncover many graces that get buried by voice mails, e-mails, and meetings.

My brother, a medical student and future surgeon, offers a helpful perspective on the gift of retrospect at the end of the day. He is very reflective and wise, so much so that sometimes I forget that he is two years younger than me. During one of our marathon phone conversations he said to me, "I rarely think about my faith when I'm at the hospital. I just don't have time during the day because I'm busy taking care of patients and trying to look good in front of the surgical team. My mind is moving so fast there isn't an opportunity to think about what I am doing."

"But," he said, "when I take a step back, maybe over the weekend or at the end of the day, I think about the families I have discharged from the hospital and the events I have participated in. I think about the fact that I comforted the mother of a baby about to undergo heart surgery, or that I developed a relationship with a guy who is dying of complications from hepatitis C. I didn't really reflect on these relationships while they were going on, didn't think of myself as having looked to my faith for guiding principles. Yet it is when I take a step back that I tend to look at my job through the eyes of faith, that I am struck by how fortunate I was to have been a part of certain situations.

"It's kind of like some of the scenes in the movie *The Matrix*," he said. "Keanu Reeves has never been one who is good with words, but there is a point in the movie where he uncovers the aliens who are controlling the earth and he realizes the vast powers he is up against. There is a flash of chaotic scenes, the camera zooms in just on him, and he just says in awe, "Whhhooaa." It is a single line in the midst of a scene of chaos, but it pretty much sums up how I feel when I reflect on my workday. I just feel a real sense of awe."

When we look back at the end of the day, it is not simply memory that is the goal. Memory in and of itself leaves us in the past, whereas reflecting intentionally and gratefully gives us courage for the future and encourages us to look at tomorrow with an open heart. The hope is to look at the day with a sense of graced understanding, to see one's life through the eyes of faith. There's a long history in our tradition of seeing and hearing God in our day-to-day experiences. If we can't find God within the boundaries of a twenty-four-hour day, what other options do we have?

Someone once recommended a practice to me that I've tried to undertake, at certain times anyway, to be more conscious about retrospect and graced understanding. In my current job there is a time of year that is extremely busy: from February until April. (I suppose it's the same for accountants as the tax day deadline nears.) During these dreary months I work a lot of weekends and evenings, and events seem to approach so quickly, one after the other, with no breathing room in between. I often feel like I can lift my head up only far enough to see what is right in front of me. At this point during the year I feel that I need all of the "graced understanding" I can get.

I found that each year, from February to April, I developed an incredibly negative attitude during these months and was probably a real downer to be around, both at the office and at home. Finally, I decided that I wasn't going to be that way anymore. I thought back to a suggested practice I had heard about once of writing down three to five blessings from your day, things that you are grateful for. I kept up this practice during my difficult months, and I was amazed at what a difference it made. I felt gratitude for things I had previously overlooked: the opportunity to have lunch with a friend, a funny e-mail from a co-worker, a presentation that had gone really well. After a couple of months of trying to cultivate this "attitude of gratitude," I experienced a real shift in perspective. I noticed that I would even approach the beginning of the day as if I were on the lookout for the good things instead of waiting until the end of the day to find them.

Keeping a "gratitude list" helped me get through those difficult months. I don't keep a list all the time, but I keep my spiral-bound notebook close at hand so it will be accessible when I need to pull it out again. As a result of this practice, I look upon the end of the day differently now. I am, of course, still glad that my workday is over, and I see the day coming to a close as an opportunity to reflect for a little while.

Little Calls, Great Results

It seems to be easier in some careers than others to see the connections between faith and work. For physicians, high school teachers, social workers, or those otherwise involved in what are often classified as "helping professions," it is easier to look upon one's work as a mission. But what about a field that's not typically looked upon as a helping profession? I asked a friend of mine who recently started teaching engineering at a Big Ten university about this issue. As he began his first semester there, he was fresh out of a doctoral program, educated, energetic, and ready to go. Upon arriving at his new job he found out that, being the new kid on the block, he had been assigned to teach a class that all the students hated — one of those prerequisites that everybody just wants to get out of the way. In addition, his students were typical second-semester seniors: antsy, plagued by incurable spring fever, and ready to graduate. The class had the scintillating title of "Measurements Lab." Luckily he had to teach it for only a semester. He spent a lot of time preparing the lectures and decided that, even though no one (including him) thought the material was interesting, he was going to teach it as well as he could.

He's finished teaching the class now and glad to be done. "Of course," he said, "it's hard to find any direct connection between the actual material that I'm teaching and my faith. But I hope the way I treated the students indicated that I was a person of faith. I cared about how they fared in my class. I left my office door open so they knew I was available for help, which is not something that all professors do. I made sure I learned all their names. My faith manifests itself in how I treat my students." Certainly this is an excellent way to connect your faith and work: to treat those around you with compassion and care, even when you may not be thrilled about your specific responsibilities.

For another friend of mine, integrating his faith and work involves bringing an ethical perspective into his work environment. He is a television producer and has worked on all kinds of shows. He's written scripts on everything from blizzards to bounty hunters to unconventional warfare. When I asked him about how his faith and work fit together, he spoke of that connection as something that he continually struggles with. He expressed some frustration that his company "didn't have a more explicit sense of mission."

He struggles with the fact that he works for the media, a business that is rarely looked upon as having a positive influence on society. He wrestles with the fact that much of what the media does is not lifegiving. "We can try to write off the media and say that the media is evil, but we can't just get rid of it, because it is such an integral part of culture. As far as the media is concerned I feel like I just have to separate the wheat from the chaff, because no matter what, the media is going to be there." He talked about how it is his faith that allows him to separate the wheat from the chaff, to look at his work critically, asking the question when filming certain subject matter, "Is this ethical?" He added, "My faith is what makes me ask, 'Is this lifegiving?'"

His faith is what gives him both an ethical perspective and the impetus to treat both his co-workers and his filming subjects with dignity. This manifested itself on one occasion when he traveled to Russia to film a show on submarine espionage during the Cold War. While he was there he interviewed a woman whose husband had died on a submarine, and as he questioned her she completely broke down and cried. "A lot of people wanted to include that part in the show, but I really discouraged it," he said. "It was a matter of acknowledging her human dignity."

While his faith doesn't always manifest itself explicitly, occasionally it does come up in conversation. "One time," he said, "I spent three and a half months working on a one-hour show on blizzards for The Weather Channel, and I thought to myself, 'What good is coming from this?' Surprisingly enough, it was while working on the blizzard show that I ended up having a really deep conversation about faith and ethics with a young woman who was one of the editors. She was really surprised that I thought about those kinds of things. It's good to be in a secular workplace and still have the opportunity to share this perspective."

My producer-friend summed it up really well when he said, "I may not be making a huge, sweeping impact like those who decide what is going to be on *60 Minutes,* but I definitely feel like I'm making a contribution to society by having my voice out there and making little calls." We all have the opportunity during our workdays to make little calls, to ask that provocative question, to be a voice for human dignity, to separate the wheat from the chaff within the bounds of our occupation.

What about those of us who work in huge corporations? The corporate world is often considered the work environment with the biggest moral void. Success is marked by enormous profits, a forty-hour workweek is nonexistent, and greed often runs rampant. So how does faith fit in with those who work in corporate America? Is living as a moral person in the business world just a nice idea? For many years it was a commonly held belief that faith and fortune don't mix, but in recent years bringing spirituality into the workplace has become less taboo. The cover story in a recent issue of *Fortune* magazine entitled "God and Business" was devoted to the groundswell of support behind bringing spirituality into the workplace in Corporate America. The juxtaposition of the words "God" and "Business" looked so unusual that I did a double take when I breezed by the magazine rack in the grocery store. If *Fortune* magazine is any sort of cultural indicator, though, it looks like faith is working its way into the business world, too.

As twenty-somethings we are both blessed and cursed by being the youngest members in the work force. We have the most energy and the least amount of experience. Often we possess the most idealism and the lowest level of jadedness. Because of our unique position in society, we have a responsibility to be a source of new life in our workplaces, even when it's hard. I've been encouraged in my own workplace by how much older adults love being around younger people. I've been heartened by how many times I've been asked my opinion. Older adults are often quite curious about how young adults think, though they may also readily admit to not being able to understand our generation. Sometimes their curiosity is encouraging and sometimes it is a little bit aggravating. I remember talking about older co-workers with my roommates one evening as we rehashed our Thursday over chips and salsa at our kitchen table. My roommates teach at an elementary school and occasionally complain about their lunchtime conversations with the older teachers in the teachers lounge. "They are always asking me what I did over the weekend, if I went out, if I had a date. It drives me crazy," one of them said. I laughed and nodded, thinking of how much that story mirrored my own experience in my office. It confirmed my observation that older adults really *like* being around young adults. Our idealism and energy can be of benefit to any workplace, even if we don't happen to love everything about our job. Our very presence and our fresh perspectives can be a contribution.

One of the other difficulties about being new to the work force is that we may have to take jobs we don't like in order to get where we want to be someday. Just as our parents did, most of us need to climb the ladder. I was reminded of this when I was having dinner with some of my dad's college friends after a football game one weekend. One of them asked me how my job was going. "It's going pretty well," I said, trying to sound upbeat and positive. "It's a good first job." He picked up on that comment immediately. He nodded his head knowingly and laughed. "Ahh," he said, "first jobs." It was a perceptive comment from someone who had been there, someone who had climbed the ladder of success by stepping on rungs of first jobs.

So what's the best way to handle those "first jobs"? Sometimes all we can do is ensure that we are doing quality work. It sounds trite to say "Just do your best," but there is something to be said for doing things well, even if we're performing the most tedious tasks in the world. Anne Lamott, in her book *Bird by Bird,* says it very well: "You can either set brick as a laborer or as an artist. You can make the work a chore or you can have a good time. You can do it the way you used to do the dishes when you were thirteen, or you can do it as a Japanese person would perform a tea ceremony, with a level of concentration and care in which you can lose yourself, and so in which you can find yourself." Even if all you do all day is type and FedEx, type with perfection and FedEx everything on time, even early. People appreciate and notice quality work.

Even when we get past our "first jobs" and land our dream position, we may become disillusioned after a while. Our dream career suddenly isn't all that we had made it out to be. And yet we are conscious of aphorisms like the oft-quoted "Choose a job you love, and you will never have to work a day in your life," and can't help but wonder if we've chosen the right job.

Do you have to love your job all the time? Even most of the time? Some people do have to take certain jobs for economic reasons, but ideally we strive to do work that both fulfills us personally and meets a need in our society. My first job after college was a wake-up call in this regard. I was living in Seattle at the time and had a forty-five minute commute to my job, which added an extra two hours to my workday. Because of my commute, I was either at work or on my way to or from work ten hours a day. This was a real shock on the heels of my leisurely college life. Gone were the carefree days of playing Frisbee on the quad on Friday afternoons and waking up an hour before my ten-o'clock class.

Though my commute was long, some fantastic scenery accompanied my drive. As I crossed the floating bridges that stretched over Lake Washington I could look down and see that the water was dotted with boats. If I looked really carefully I could see Bill Gates's enormous compound and surrounding property. On the way to work in the morning I watched the sun rise over the Cascade Mountains, and on the way home I watched the sun set over the Olympic Mountains and the glittering waters of Puget Sound.

Driving during those sunrises and sunsets was such a gift. Even if I was stuck in traffic, the amazing backdrop made me more reflective than I otherwise would have been as I gazed at the endless trail of red brake lights in front of me. I remember thinking to myself as I commuted between mountain ranges and reflected on career options: "You'd better *like* what you end up doing for a living because you're going to spend a *lot* of time doing it." It was on those long drives that I realized that I didn't want to spend my life waiting for the end of the day to roll around, living only for the weekends. There is far too much life to be lived and enjoyed in between. Strive to find work that you like.

It is energizing to talk with my friends about our work because we've all landed in careers that we enjoy, most days. Among the group of us that have stayed in touch since college there is a psychiatrist, an entomologist, an engineer, a child life specialist, and a special education teacher. I love to hear about my friends' careers and feel fortunate to have friends who have interesting and diverse jobs and interests. To compare our lives now is bittersweet and exciting, because we have gone in very different directions since we all lived on the same campus.

I've noticed that as our career paths diverge, so do our financial decisions. It slowly becomes apparent that we've each chosen to handle our money differently. Some of us are homeowners and some are not. Some choose to take exotic trips around the world and some still live at home with their parents. Some are still in graduate school and living off of that oh-so-generous graduate student stipend and others have been out in the corporate world making a bundle since the day after graduation.

It is primarily when we get together for weddings that our different lifestyle choices come up in conversation. I remember one wedding weekend when we all went out for brunch and the conversation turned to cars. One of my friends told a funny story about how on the same day she had both lost her wedding ring and ruined the seat of the car her husband usually drives. She had left a pen in her back pocket without the cap on. By the time she realized that the uncapped pen was still in her back pocket, there was an intricate pen drawing on the leather seat of their Lexus. You could almost see the eyebrows go up around the table when she said the word "Lexus." Nobody said anything at the time, but on the way out of the restaurant one of my friends grabbed my arm. "My *dad* can't even afford a Lexus," she said.

This was just one of many indications that we've all started to establish different priorities with our money. I have one friend who can't stand any sort of chain store. She chastises us for shopping at bookstores that aren't independently run, and whenever we go out to eat she never fails to throw in a comment about how she'd like to eat at a *locally owned place,* please. Yet even with our different financial priorities, there exists that core of friendship that continues to bind us together. We will always have the comfort of shared history, the deep understanding that comes from knowing each other's families, accepting each other's faults, and appreciating each other's talents.

We don't discuss financial issues as freely as we once did in college. There are elements in our discussions of money that will always remain private. Perhaps that is something unique to American society. Sharon Dalosz Parks, in the book *Practicing Our Faith,* remarks:

> In casual conversation, it may be mentioned that "we got a good deal" or "found it on sale" or even "decided we couldn't afford it at this point." Yet a visitor from another country observed that in the United States, he might in the course of casual conversation during a car ride be told the details of the car owner's forthcoming surgical operation, but he would be far less likely to be told (and it would be rude to ask) how much the car cost or how much the owner makes. In the domain of economic life, we typically remain strangers to one another — each of us essentially alone with our sense of busyness and cumber, fear and guilt.

There will always be the element of privacy that accompanies any discussion of money, but money, like it or not, remains at the center of our thoughts as we attempt to find our place in the working world. Emerging differences in the handling of money and choices of lifestyle are a hallmark of the entrance into adulthood, and so far my friends and I have all managed to respect each other's differences and our friendship continues to grow.

Relating to Those Who Have Less

Ultimately as we journey through adulthood we also make decisions about how we're going to relate to the poor. For some of us that means working with them very directly, for some that means making a financial commitment to share our resources, and for others that will mean combining contributions of time and talent. Relating to those who have less means that, in whatever community, workplace, or geographical setting we find ourselves, we continually ask what the Rev. Richard Fragomeni refers to as the "edge" question, that is, "Who is being forgotten?" "Who is being left out of this community's life, and *why?*" Jesus said, "The poor will always be among you," and because of this, we are called to an awareness of those who are marginalized, those who, in the words of a mentor, "are not people who merely slipped through the cracks. These people were *born* in the cracks."

I've seen my friends care for the poor in a variety of ways. One would periodically spend the night at a men's homeless shelter, giving the gift of his presence and time. "It was something I could do very easily, being single," he said. "It was a shift that very few people could work." Another acquaintance continues to give money to an Appalachian mission she worked at on a college spring break. My former college roommate teaches computer skills to men and women who live in low-income areas.

My own contributions have shifted throughout the years. When I was in graduate school I used to work very regularly at the local homeless shelter and am grateful for those experiences. Now I work full-time, and devoting that amount of time to the homeless is not feasible anymore. I've chosen to share my resources through the opportunities in my own workplace: cutting up fresh vegetables for the guests at a men's homeless shelter, buying gifts for foster children whose names are on our parish "Giving Tree," donating money to the Sudanese refugee family in my parish.

Sometimes helping the poor means speaking out on their behalf. One stellar example is Sr. Helen Prejean. During her commencement speech at my college graduation, she spoke passionately about the death row inmates she had spent time with. She became a spiritual advisor to many of them, prayed with them, and sometimes witnessed their executions. She spoke of the connection between poverty and the death penalty. Referring to the first death row inmate she met, she said, "Before I even knew him I knew that he was on death row *because he was poor,* and that was enough to get started." Since hearing her inspiring address I've tried to read more about capital punishment and why the Catholic Church is so staunchly opposed. I speak out against the death penalty whenever I give a presentation on Catholic social teaching and talk about how it violates the dignity of human life. I'm still learning, but from Sr. Helen I've caught a glimpse of what an impact one can make by being an advocate for the poor.

Caring for the poor, integrating our faith and work, making responsible financial decisions — all these issues provide much food for thought. It will take a lifetime to plumb the depths of meaning that our work can have, to discern how in our work we can build up the kingdom of God and reflect God's unconditional love. We're already doing it, in our day-to-day lives and daily routines, and yet we haven't even tapped into most of our potential. We're *already* doing what we are called to do but have *not yet* even scratched the surface. We've discovered the first inklings of what our calling may be — through the affirmation of a co-worker who says, "You're really good at this" or a student of ours who really "gets it" for the first time. And yet it will take a lifetime to figure out how to be faithful to our calling, our vocation, in whatever our career may be. Young adulthood is the perfect time to start. We've got time on our side.

❧ *Six* ❧

Community Matters

*Community is the place where the person
you least want to live with lives.*

—Henri Nouwen

Community is about living with the people that we love.

—Rev. Nicholas Ayo, C.S.C.

One of my earliest experiences of community as a young adult took place immediately after my graduation from college. I had joined a post-graduate service program in Seattle that trains and supports young college graduates in social service or parish positions. There were twelve of us in the year-long program, and we all began our experience in the summer with a three-week orientation program. Part of the program was the "housing process," a discernment program designed to assist the group in deciding who was to live together. The program staff determined early on that our group would be divided into two separate households. As you can imagine, the living arrangements quickly became the hot topic of our conversations. The question, "Who do you think you want to live with?" dominated our discussions during the first few days we were together. We were practically strangers at this point and were continually sizing each other up, silently making judgments about whom we did and didn't want to live with for the year.

Two weeks into our time together, the much-anticipated "housing process" began. We had to write on scraps of paper the names of the three people we most wanted to live with, and if there was anyone we were absolutely positive we couldn't live with, we had to write that person's name down too. I really felt like I could live with anyone in the program except for one person. That person's name was Benjamin. I barely knew him, but I was completely bothered by him for a number of reasons. My mental litany of strikes against him was long. He came from a very wealthy family and at the age of twenty-seven had never gone grocery shopping or written a personal check. He had literally been waited on for his entire life up to this point and had very few practical skills as a result.

His lack of independence bothered me, and, in addition, his understanding of faith didn't seem to fit very well with mine. In our summer orientation program he never said a word during any of our small group discussions on service, community, and justice. His spirituality was very black-and-white, almost fundamentalist, and did not allow any room for the opinions of those of us who liked to identify some gray areas. Benjamin did not sleep at night and spent the evenings pacing the floor of our residence hall, reading Scripture as he walked. He once lashed out at one of our guest speakers with a vengeance that was almost scary. He chain-smoked too. My mental list of judgments and strikes against him was long, and my sense of self-righteousness emerged in full force.

As you can probably guess, despite my request not to live with Benjamin, I was placed in a house with him. I was mortified and angered that the directors of our program had not heeded my explicit request not to live with him. This was someone I was going to see every day, someone whom I was going to be sharing a living room, kitchen, and bathroom with, someone with whom I would be spending major holidays. Out of twelve possible people, I had been placed with the one person I had requested not to live with. The words of Henri Nouwen played over and over again in my mind, "Community is the place where the person you least want to live with lives." The first time I heard this quote in a video I found it slightly amusing, yet when the quote became a reality in my own life I didn't find it the least bit funny. I was annoyed and worried.

I thought about the prospect of living with Benjamin for a long time and eventually decided not to question the decision of the program staff — primarily because I was thrilled about the other three people whom I had been placed with: Jen, Kat, and Bill. During the three weeks of orientation I had found them to be fun, faith-filled, and very genuine people — people I wanted to get to know better.

So the five of us found a house and moved in, and things went pretty much as I expected. Jen and Kat and I got along beautifully and did everything together. We hiked in the mountains almost every weekend, explored the city of Seattle, and stayed up late talking most nights. Bill and I got along too, and although he wasn't around much, I always enjoyed talking to him, usually as he concocted one of his vegetarian specialties in our kitchen. The four of us supported each other in the ups and downs of our new jobs and shared household responsibilities — grocery shopping, cleaning, paying bills — very equally, for the most part.

Of course, I avoided contact with Benjamin whenever possible. I turned down his invitations to go to dinner and cringed every time I drove home from work and saw his car in the driveway. Looking back, I realize that I began the whole year with a very mean-spirited attitude toward him. With my judgmental nature out in full force, Benjamin didn't stand a chance.

He continually did things that tried my patience and the patience of everyone else in the house. He sometimes didn't come home when it was his night to cook dinner. It would take him two hours to go grocery shopping because he had never done it before and he got lost in the aisles. He never quite could figure out a personal check, which sometimes caused our rent money to be late. He couldn't seem to hold down a job — he went through three or four social service positions and was fired from each one.

The culmination of my uneasiness with Benjamin came when he offered to pick me up from the Seattle airport one day after I had just spent the fourth of July holiday with my boyfriend's family. Initially I was grateful for his offer. But I had barely picked up my bags from the baggage claim when Benjamin said that he had done a lot of thinking and he thought we should start dating. I became completely uncomfortable at this point and told him that I thought it was absurd. From that day until the day I moved out of the house,

I expended even more energy avoiding Benjamin. I was rude to him and short with him when he spoke to me.

Three weeks after the airport incident, the time came for me to move back to the Midwest to begin graduate school. I was the first in my Seattle community to leave, and I said goodbye to Benjamin cordially and quickly. I was sad to say goodbye to the rest of my community but was grateful to be free from the sometimes awkward day-to-day interactions with Benjamin.

A few days after I had moved back to the Midwest, I received a phone call from one of my housemates, still in Seattle. She called with shocking news. They had discovered that Benjamin was a diagnosed schizophrenic. He had evidently moved out to Seattle without telling anyone of his illness and had not taken his prescription medication in nearly a year. Evidently, after I had moved out he had had an absolute breakdown and had confessed all of this to Jen, Kat, and Bill. He was now in the process of packing up his things and moving back to his hometown in Ohio to get some help and to start the road to recovery.

Hearing of Benjamin's mental illness, I suddenly felt very weak and strange. All of a sudden, it all started to make sense: the strange behavior, the inability to hold a job, the struggles with writing personal checks, the difficulty relating to his housemates. All of these occurrences were warning signals the rest of us should have paid more attention to. As I replayed all of Benjamin's strange antics and behaviors in my head, all the details came together to form a coherent picture.

After I got over the shock of Benjamin's news, I began to realize that in the midst of all my mean-spiritedness, self-centeredness, and judgmental tendencies, I had missed an opportunity within my small community. I had missed a call to compassion. Benjamin was that call. Perhaps God was calling me, through Benjamin, through the community, to be more compassionate and less judgmental.

I began to feel very guilty later. All of Benjamin's habits that I had mentally lashed out against were in fact cries for help. If only I had thought critically enough about his situation to ask, "Why?" "Why is he like this?" If only I had turned outward for a moment and reached out to him. Throughout the entire year I had hardly heeded the advice of the ancient Jewish philosopher Philo of Alexandria: "Be kind, for everyone you meet is fighting a great battle." I had not taken to heart the words of the honorable Atticus Finch in the novel *To Kill a Mockingbird,* who admonished his daughter Scout never to judge people until she had walked a mile in their shoes. Not only had I never walked a mile in Benjamin's shoes, I had never even for a moment dared to try them on. I rarely even allowed myself to look in his direction.

I often wonder what would have happened if I had opened my heart to Benjamin; if I had opened my mind to him; if I had not avoided him; if I had abandoned my self-righteous mannerisms and behaviors. I wondered if he would have told me about his illness had I taken the time for him. I will always wonder what things would have been like if I had answered his call to compassion. I wonder what gifts he would have brought out in me, and what gifts I would have discovered in him.

Benjamin called me a few weeks later, just I had started graduate school in the Midwest. He apologized for never telling us about his illness, and told me that he missed our community very much. Our conversation was very short, but it provided the closure I needed. How ironic that it was Benjamin who took the initiative to be the peacemaker in the end.

Well over six months after I spoke with Benjamin, I ate dinner with a priest friend of mine and told him the story of Benjamin and my Seattle community. I repeated the Henri Nouwen quote, that "community is the place where the person you least want to live with lives," and my friend grew thoughtful. "I know what Nouwen means," said Fr. Ayo, "But community is also inclusive of the people we love. It is important not to lose sight of that. Community is surely just as much about living with the people we cherish and whose company we truly enjoy." Wise and hopeful words, indeed. I thought about my love for those other members in my community, Jen, Kat, and Bill, and realized that my relationships with them were just as representative of authentic community as was my difficult relationship with Benjamin.

Community Calls

I feel fortunate to have been a part of many communities that have both comforted and challenged me. A variety of communities has been instrumental in the discernment of my own vocation. Though the discernment of a vocation certainly has an individual, personal dimension, we live out our vocation within the context of community and receive our vocational calls from within the various groups of which we are a part: institutions, organizations, neighborhoods, families, circles of friends, cities, states, churches, and nations. All the communities we belong to, however loosely or tightly we may be affiliated with them, play a role in the cultivation, stimulation, and growth of our vocation.

Sometimes the role of a community may be as simple and basic as providing a safe and nurturing environment, an environment that lays a solid foundation of values and experiences to draw upon at a later time. I think back to my childhood neighborhood as this kind of setting. My family lived in a residential area where there were five or six families that all lived within a mile of each other. Each family had groups of kids who were all about the same age. We spent hours, days, and years growing up together. In the winter we skied and sledded for days on end, and in the summer we swam and rode our bikes together. We spent the night at each other's houses when the electrical power went out during Michigan's fiercest winter storms and ice skated on an ice rink that a group of dads built in a couple of backyards. We laughed and celebrated together, mostly, but we also cried together, when deaths occurred and when families endured illness, the care of aging relatives, and other difficulties. This large "extended family" has even established a few of its own traditions, my favorite of which takes place on Thanksgiving every year.

Each Thanksgiving morning at about nine o'clock, a sleepy but determined crew gathers on the street corner for the annual four-mile run/walk, the "Turkey Trot," as it has come to be called. A hokey Midwestern tradition it may be, but a serious tradition it has become. Gradually, smilingly, people of all ages clad in running gear, sweatpants, and jeans reunite in the chilly morning air. Most of us "kids," who are now in our twenties, haven't seen each other in a year, so there are lots of hugs and catch-up conversations: "How do you like your job?" "Are you still dating that guy?" "How long are you home for?" "Can't wait for your wedding!"

The conversation continues as our group, usually twenty or thirty strong, makes its way along the four-mile Turkey Trot course, some by running or walking, some rollerblading or biking. The pace is leisurely but the conversation is lively. We tease each other about the things we used to do or say when we were kids and furtively check out the various significant others that people have brought home with them for Thanksgiving. We often joke that before someone in our crew gets married, their boyfriend, girlfriend, or fiancé has to pass the yearly neighborhood evaluation. And woe to the individual who doesn't pass the Turkey Trot test! Some boyfriends and girlfriends even actually "trained" for the event in the weeks preceding it.

The Turkey Trot always ends with a breakfast outside on my family's back patio: coffee, hot apple cider, coffee cake, and hot cinnamon apples. Some years the unseasonably balmy November weather has allowed our conversations to linger. Some years the winter weather arrives early, the cold air stings bare skin, and snow covers the ground around us, so people quickly down hot coffee and return home to put their turkeys in the oven and spend the day with extended family.

These Thanksgiving morning encounters and conversations are brief, yet there is something comforting about being able to touch base with my childhood friends, their parents, and their significant others, albeit briefly. Family structures are changing, with the introduction of spouses and new babies, and it is fun to see the neighborhood community expanding and branching out. I don't keep in touch regularly with my childhood friends by phone or by e-mail, and that is why this yearly gathering has become so important. Our morning run and ensuing meal provide a brief opportunity to touch base, to get in touch with a very significant part of my past, and this unearths memories that are both good and bad, happy and humbling.

It is during brief encounters like the one on Thanksgiving morning that I can see why Jesus once said that none of us are prophets in our own hometown. When I am home I am with the people who have seen me at my best and at my worst, and in every stage of growth in between. These are the people who will remember not only that I was usually a good kid, but also that I used to coerce younger neighborhood kids into starring in one of my ridiculous "basement theater" plays and that my neighbor friend and I founded a "bike club" that involved nothing other than riding bikes in and out of other people's driveways. These are the people who remember how I used to dress in high school and what I used to get into trouble for. They remember all the quirky and mischievous things I have done throughout the years. For these reasons it is always good to be home, and it is always very humbling to be home!

I have become grateful for these long-lasting relationships, especially during the past couple of years as I have moved farther away from home. I never knew how comforting it could be to maintain friendships with people whom I have known as long as I can remember. After moving to several different cities and towns during my twenties, I am much more appreciative of people who know what I am about, where I came from, and what my immediate family is about. I remember reading the words of one of my favorite newspaper columnists a few years ago and not quite grasping her sentiments on this matter. Mary Schmich, a metro columnist for the *Chicago Tribune* wrote: "Hang on to the people who knew you when you were young. You'll need them when you grow old." I remember at one point reading that sentence over again because initially I didn't quite get it. I knew cognitively what Schmich meant, but I never grasped it on an experiential level until recently. Though I would hardly classify myself as "old" right now, I am beginning to understand the importance of being in touch with my roots, of revisiting, both physically and emotionally, one of the first communities I ever knew.

Sometimes I wonder if I'll ever experience the kind of community that I had growing up. I've lived in three different cities since graduating from college, and I have to say that I have never really known my neighbors in any of these locations. Occasionally I would catch glimpses of them as I arrived home or as they drove up to their house, but our encounters never amounted to more than a brief "Hi." I miss having someone to give one of my house keys to in case I lock myself out of the house, or having someone close by to pick up my mail while I am out of town. I hope that the close-knit kind of community that I grew up in isn't a thing of the past. I think of recently published books like Robert Putnam's *Bowling Alone,* which lament the decline of the local community and argue that Americans are more disconnected than ever from their families, neighbors, and communities.

I realize now that the supportive and nurturing community I grew up in laid a solid foundation for the cultivation of my sense of vocation. My neighborhood "extended family," as I have come to call them, taught me, at a very basic level, the values of thoughtfulness, hospitality, generosity, support, and humor. It has helped me tremendously as I journey through adulthood to see how families live out these values in their own unique ways. In being a part of a community I learned that there are many different ways one can be generous, many ways one can offer support, many ways one can use humor to teach a lesson or make a point. We don't all have to be the same. In my continuing discernment of vocation I am glad to have experienced many examples of these values at work in a community.

In reflecting further on my Thanksgiving morning experiences over the years, I realize that what could be dismissed merely as a hokey Midwestern tradition has become a vital experience of community. Perhaps this is, in part, because our neighborhood's morning gathering includes (although we are pretty irreverent about it) all the tried-and-true strategies of the earliest Christians' celebrations and the basis for what we now refer to as the Mass or the Eucharist. The essential components of any such event: gather the people, break the bread, and tell the stories.

We don't look pretty at this Thanksgiving morning gathering. Many of us have arrived home on late flights the night before and some stayed out at the bars really late and have puffy, tired eyes to show for it. Waking up early on a holiday weekend is tough.

Waking up early on a holiday weekend to exercise in November is even tougher. Cold Midwestern temperatures necessitate layers of running gear: hats, scarves, and gloves, hardly the stuff of high fashion. We may not look good, but the point is that we are together. We have gathered. We have each made it a point to be together. It is well worth our time on a busy holiday weekend to touch base with one another.

As we run, walk, and rollerblade, we tell stories of past and present, a combination of pleasant memories, current workplace woes, and relationship successes or dilemmas. It is this sharing of stories that bonds us. It is the updating and conversing that maintain and strengthen our relationships, enough so that we will be able next year to pick up where we left off, even with a yearlong gulf of non-communication in between. Our shared history and these yearly updates are the threads that keep us woven together.

And we break the bread. Actually, the bread in this situation comes in the form of nut roll or coffee cake, but the meal is just as important as the gathering and the sharing. The dearth of leftovers at the end of the morning is a testament to the meal's importance. We return to our individual homes late in the morning on Thanksgiving reconnected, nourished, and refreshed. The community has been attended to and renewed, at least for now. We are okay for another year. Ritual has gathered us together and has nourished our relationships once more.

We Were Made for This

It is in our God-given nature to be oriented toward community. We are *imago Dei,* created in the image of God, a God whose very nature is communal. The God who created us is Father, Son, and Spirit: three persons in one God, a concept we refer to as the Trinity. The persons of the Father, Son, and Spirit are in active relationship with one another, and we are created for relationship as well. The three persons of the Trinity, a divine community in and of themselves, serve as a model of community that is in right relationship.

The three persons of the Trinity have a perfect relationship of mutual love, service, and support. In Scripture Jesus often speaks of his close relationship with the Father, especially in John's Gospel:

> Truly, truly, I say to you, the Son can do nothing of his own accord, but only what he sees the Father doing; for whatever he does, that the Son does likewise. For the Father loves the Son, and shows him all that he himself is doing; and greater works than these will he show him, that you may marvel. (John 5:19–20)

This passage illustrates the special close relationship between the Father and the Son. Another example of this closeness between Father, Son, and Spirit is when John the Baptist baptizes Jesus in the Jordan River. At the moment Jesus is baptized, the heavens break open, God sends the Spirit in the form of a dove, and God's voice from heaven says for all to hear: "This is my beloved Son; with whom I am well pleased" (Mark 1:9–11).

Father, Son, and Spirit form a close, loving, and divine community, and as *imago Dei* we are created for such community. When we succumb to the rugged individualistic tendencies of our American culture — the tendencies to separate and go at life alone — we are at odds with our God-given nature. There is room in our human nature for *both* the individual and the community, and these two natures balance and complete one another. Living out a vocation calls us to reflect inward, to listen to the voice of God within us and become the best person we can be, and it also calls us outward, to be the presence of God to others within the context of community.

At my cousin's wedding a few years ago, the best man offered a toast that I believe captures at least some of the essence of community. His toast included a quote that I have often heard at weddings: "Marriage means not only to gaze into each other's eyes but to gaze outward in the same direction." Marriage needs to be nurtured from the inside but also calls us to nurture those on the outside. Community calls us beyond the relationships that are natural, easy, comfortable to maintain. It is good when two people, through their marriage, forge a relationship that is loving and trusting, a solid foundation. Community calls a couple beyond the foundation of their marriage. It calls them to utilize that strong foundation, to build outward from it, to contribute to and to improve the community around them.

Community requires us to work for people other than ourselves, to live for people other than ourselves. Our generation is often commended for living in this way, for our commitment to alleviating poverty and working for justice. Examples abound of people our age who have committed their lives to people other than themselves, to people of other nations: social workers, Maryknoll missionaries, Peace Corps volunteers, and college graduates who commit themselves to post-graduate service programs serve as living examples of those who make community a priority. For it is on this individual level, as people made in the image of a relational God, that we transform neighborhood communities, cities, and nations. When we commit ourselves to community we commit ourselves to seeking out the needs within our human family. And the outlook for our world is bleak if we do not each commit ourselves to community. Joan Chittister conveys this idea very well in her book *Wisdom Distilled from the Daily:*

> Unless we learn in our own personal relationships, as the ancient definition of heaven and hell indicates, to live for someone besides ourselves, how shall we as a nation ever learn to hear the cries of the starving in Ethiopia and the illiterate in Africa and the refugees in the Middle East and the war weary in Central America? What will become of a nation in this day and age that has no sense of community?

The very welfare of our world is dependent upon whether or not we as individuals commit ourselves to community. This commitment can be a challenge, but it is good to remember that we are wired by our Creator for community, and we should stay true to our construction.

That there is something in our human, God-given nature that calls us to community is apparent. This innate quality is especially apparent in the face of both great joy and great tragedy. There is something deep within us that calls us to come together in the face of disaster and death. Never has this been so apparent to our generation as it was on September 11, 2001, when groups of terrorists flew jetliners into the twin towers of the World Trade Center, the side of the Pentagon, and a remote field in Pennsylvania.

At the time of the attacks I was working at a large parish just outside of Dayton, Ohio. For most of the day my co-workers and I sat, dazed, as everyone did, in front of the television and watched the twin towers crumble, over and over again. Shock gave way to anger, and anger to sadness. For a few hours we seemed to move about our office like ghosts. Eventually we realized that we needed to do something — we needed to provide an opportunity for people to come together to pray. A few of us from the staff met in the afternoon to decide what we would offer to support our church community in the face of such tragedy. We tossed a few ideas around and eventually decided to have a Mass that evening. We were at a loss as to what would be appropriate in this situation. We pulled out all of the resources that were available to us and found that there is a special Mass for Times of War and Civil Disturbance and special prayers of blessing for victims of terrible crimes. We barely had enough time to get the word out to people that we were having Mass that evening. We sent out a barrage of e-mails, organized some phone chains, and notified the local television and radio stations.

Despite the short notice, the attendance that night was remarkable. Our church filled with people, and they sang with an intensity and urgency, a strength of prayer that I had never heard before. People of all ages gathered, some with young children who were asleep in their parents' arms. After Mass, many people expressed their gratitude for the opportunity to come together. We found comfort and strength in the presence of our faith community in the face of tragedy. There was something deep within us that drew us outward, toward each other on the evening of September 11. Though the newspaper headlines and articles in the ensuing weeks continually reminded readers that "the world is a dangerous, dangerous place," I kept thinking of the faith-filled community gathered at St. Charles that September evening and couldn't help but think otherwise.

Especially in these times, we are called to reclaim our communities, to make our communities life-giving environments rather than places where we live in fear. In thinking about a life-giving environment I recall a scene from the Terry Gilliam film *The Fisher King,* which illustrates this point. The two main characters, Parry (Robin Williams) and Jack (Jeff Bridges), decide to spend an evening together. Their wanderings take them to Central Park, which is dark, save for the city lights and the full moon. Their conversation about the safety of a dark Central Park reveals the two characters' differing perspectives on community:

Parry: What a beautiful night, Jack!

Jack: Don't you think it's time to go now? Running around here during the day is one thing, but at night we could be killed by a wide variety of people.

Parry: That's stupid Jack. I mean, this park is mine just as much as it is theirs. Do you think it's fair that they can keep us out just by making us think we might get killed?

Jack: I think it's very fair.

Parry: Well, I don't.

After this conversation, Parry settles in on the wide expanse of grass under the full moon in Central Park, claiming it for his own as a place of goodness and beauty instead of one of danger and darkness. And this very action of Parry's is what we are called to do. Community calls us to create places of safety and beauty, even if that requires that we reclaim them from those who would prefer dens of darkness and danger.

Sit in the Front Row

True community calls us to participation. Community calls us to sit in the front row, to fully engage ourselves. I recently attended a summer conference on a college campus and decided to have lunch with a friend before the afternoon keynote session. We were deeply engrossed in conversation, and I checked my watch toward the end of the lunch and realized that I was going to be late for the afternoon session. But I was really involved in our conversation and enjoying the catch-up time with my friend. So I made a silent decision that I would be just a few minutes late for the session and quietly slip into the back row of the auditorium.

I arrived at the auditorium about ten minutes late, and the room was completely silent as the audience listened to the speaker. I scanned the back rows for an empty seat, but I couldn't find one anywhere. Fine, I thought, I'll just lean against the back wall and no one will notice. But no such luck. A determined, wholesome-looking woman with a giant nametag that said "Conference Coordinator" strode purposefully toward me. I desperately pretended not to see her, but to no avail. "We've got one more seat left," she said. "Great, I appreciate that," I said thankfully, scanning the back rows again, looking for the one empty seat. "It's right up in the front row," she said, grabbing my arm. Before I could protest she led me up the side aisle, right in front of the hundreds of people in the auditorium, to a seat right in front of the keynote speaker. Served me right for extending my lunch by a few minutes!

I was pretty mortified for a little while, but eventually I settled in and listened to the speaker, who turned out to be extraordinarily dynamic and articulate. I was captivated by her talk, in part because she was right in front of me. I diligently took notes during the whole address, not because I had to, but because I was so interested and inspired by what she had to say.

I realize now that I would not have gleaned as much from the keynote address if I had continued to lean against the back of the auditorium wall for the entire hour, as I had originally planned. Since I sat front and center, though against my will, I became completely absorbed in the experience. In turn I now have some wisdom to share and put to good use in my workplace, wisdom that I probably wouldn't have picked up on had I stayed in the back of the enormous auditorium. I was glad, in this case, that I was forced to participate. I suppose I should thank the woman with the "Conference Coordinator" nametag. I reaped the benefits of being in a little community with her, even if it was just for a couple of hours.

Though our human nature sometimes tempts us to sit in the back row, fostering a bit of apathy and nonparticipation, it is good, most of the time, to sit up front, both literally and figuratively. "Sitting up front" is a good metaphor for what is required of us in community. Not all of us are born leaders, and not all of us are comfortable enough to sit up front and raise our hands, but we are all, at the very least, called to participation. Community calls us to engage fully with those around us. So vote. Care. Have an opinion. Express an opinion. Take on a new project. Get involved. These are just different ways of saying the same thing. To be an authentic member of the Christian community is to participate and share our gifts.

Community calls us to share our gifts in order to transform our communities. We all have a different assortments of gifts, different combinations. We discern and develop our gifts both individually and communally, in the hope that we can share them with others. Some people are incredible writers, some are innovative business leaders, and some are compassionate caregivers. Our gifts have to do with our professional skills, our industriousness, our talents, and our intellectual prowess, but our gifts must be understood from a broader perspective as well.

Many of us think that to share our gifts, we have to *do* things. We value productivity and tangible, visible results and thus equate these with sharing our gifts. We are raised on the Nike mantra "Just do it." I classify myself as an obsessive doer. I like to be constantly busy and become uncomfortable when I have my hands free for even a few minutes. For a long time I equated sharing my gifts with being busy all the time and having multiple commitments. In my mind, I wasn't making an adequate contribution to the world if I had too much spare time on my hands.

My preoccupation with "doing" became especially apparent when I cooked dinner with a friend one night. We decided to make some chicken and pasta, and I threw a handful of spaghetti in a pot of water to boil. I read the pasta package and saw that the spaghetti needed to cook for twelve minutes. "Well," I said to my friend, "what are we going to *do* while we wait for this pasta to boil?" As soon as the words were out of my mouth I realized how ridiculous I sounded. My friend laughed and shook his head. "Why don't we just stay here in the kitchen and talk. Let's just enjoy being together." Just enjoy being together, I thought. What a novel concept. Sometimes it takes another person for us to recognize our tendencies and idiosyncrasies — another benefit of community! Since my friend and I cooked dinner that night, I have been more aware of my preoccupation with "doing" and have tried to be more comfortable merely sitting still and enjoying another person's company.

Our gifts can be charisms just as much as they can be specific skills, as Rev. Richard Fragomeni writes in his book *Come to the Feast*. The seven gifts of the Holy Spirit are not specific skills, like organization or technological savvy, but are better classified as charisms, qualities that require a certain way of *being* rather than *doing:* wisdom, understanding, courage, awe, good judgment, strength, and holiness. We don't have to *do* anything to be wise or courageous or appreciative. Sometimes the sharing of gifts involves nothing more than showing faith and courage in the face of adversity or displaying generosity with the length of our attention span for a friend who needs a good listener.

The sharing of gifts can be a source of great joy. When we are truly sharing our gifts, our work seems almost effortless. The reason people burn out from their jobs is that they are not employed in ways that properly harness their talents and charisms.

Why Go to Church?

In any discussion of community it is good to talk about the role of a faith community as well. Why be a part of one in the first place? Why go to church at all? I asked a professor this question once, expecting to hear the usual answers: attending church keeps you accountable; going to Mass instills good values, and (even better!) receiving Communion forgives all your sins for the week to come. But his answer really surprised me. "The church really needs you," he said simply. *The church needs me.* The church needs my gifts. The church needs my talents.

Although this reason is not the only compelling one for belonging to a faith community, it is a good one. I had always thought of Mass in terms of what I got out of it. For many years I would walk into church, usually a different church each week, depending on my mood, and sit in the back, my defiant mindset guiding my mental conversation. Silently, inwardly, I'd say to the presiding priest: Go ahead. Impress me with your homily. Inspire me. Give me a tidbit of wisdom I can take home for the week. Try, just try, to relate to my life experience just once. To the choir: Sing some of the songs I like. And try to get the notes right for once. Entertain me, inspire me. To the ushers: Please, please do not ask me to bring up the gifts. I don't want to walk up the aisle in front of all these people I don't even know. Never had I thought of the whole Sunday experience in terms of what I could contribute to it. Never had I thought that perhaps my presence could make a difference to other people.

Our faith communities need us. They need the insights, energy, and experience of younger generations. We are not just the future of the church. Our generation is its present reality, and because of this we have a responsibility to participate. Our church will be better for it.

Our civic communities need us too, and so do the Benjamins of the world, no matter how much they bother us and get under our skin. So go ahead. Reach out. Get involved. Be ready to encounter both the people you love and the people you least want to be with. Recognize the calls to compassion. Be mindful that our call to community comes from places outside our nation's boundaries. There is room for everyone in God's kingdom, the ultimate community. It's a big, big place. It is time to do your part.

Seven

Mentors and Models

When you walk, they will lead you;
When you lie down, they will watch over you;
And when you awake, they will talk with you.
For the commandment is a lamp and the teaching a light.

—Proverbs 6:22–23

My favorite movie is the relatively well-known Indiana high school basketball flick *Hoosiers*. It is the only movie I own on video and the only one I have watched more than ten times. Occasionally I'll watch a snippet of it during the few minutes before I go to bed. The story gets better every time I watch it. In the film's dramatic finale, the small-town Hickory Huskers beat the South Bend Bearcats in a clincher of a game to win the Indiana basketball state finals. Even though I've watched this video countless times, I still hold my breath until Jimmy Chitwood sinks the jumper at the buzzer.

One of the reasons I like *Hoosiers* so much is that the underdogs, the good guys, win in the end. It's a classic feel-good, David and Goliath story. But the main reason I love this movie is that I admire the character of the coach, Norman Dale, played by Gene Hackman. He is a coach and mentor par excellence. Initially he breaks the players down through rigorous conditioning drills and harsh rules about passing the ball. "My practices aren't for your enjoyment," he reminds them when they resist the rigor of the workouts. Eventually he builds up his players through challenges and encouragement and draws out their maximum potential. During his first season Coach Dale accomplishes the unthinkable: He brings an eight-man team from an unknown hamlet in Indiana to the high school basketball state finals in Indianapolis.

When he and his team arrive at the Butler Fieldhouse in the state capital, looks of awe and anxiety flash across the players' faces. The athletic facility is enormous. They're not in their dusky cracker box gym in Hickory anymore. The fieldhouse holds thousands of people and is of a quality these corn-fed boys have never seen. Immediately Coach Dale takes his team under the hoop and invites them to measure the distance from the free throw line to the basket. A player measures — fifteen feet, just like at their high school gym at home in Hickory. Then Coach Dale asks another player to measure the distance from the rim to the floor — ten feet, just like at home in Hickory.

This poignant scene is my favorite part of the movie, because it shows that Coach Dale was in touch with what was on his players' minds. He knew what their fears and needs would be even before they started to practice, and he did what he needed to do to put them at ease. Coach Dale knew that being a coach required far more than conditioning drills and play calling.

A Few Good Men

I've been lucky to have some good mentors myself. When I decided to play the flute at the age of eight I was introduced to a university professor who would teach me the finer points of being a flautist until I left for college. He was a brilliant musician and a disarming and witty mentor. He ensured that I knew the importance of practicing my technical exercises and scales ad infinitum, and drilled me during my half-hour music lessons. Then, for a treat at the end of a session, he would select a duet from a Broadway play that we could play together. (He pulled out these same duets when, on many occasions, it became apparent that I hadn't practiced any of the music I was supposed to.)

He guided me through the changes I had to make when the orthodontist put braces on my teeth and later helped me again with the necessary adjustments when the braces later came off. He showed me the best kind of Chap Stick to use when my lips got chapped in the winter and interfered with my musical tone. He offered all this advice and guidance with an incredibly apparent love for life and for his profession. He spoke of the importance of sharing his musical gifts with those in his Methodist congregation on Sundays and encouraged me to do the same at my church. Though many would consider him an academic, he never lost sight of the importance of sharing his gifts with the wider community beyond the university where he taught. It was obvious that participation in his church community was important to him.

Most importantly, Dr. Osborne taught me as much about embracing life with joy as he did about playing the flute. He had (and still has) the deepest laugh, a laugh that provoked a smile from me even on the grumpiest of my teenage days. He has been married to his wife for fifty years, a milestone that they recently celebrated with their children and grandchildren in the mountains of Colorado. Though he is now in his mid-seventies he still hikes a segment of the Appalachian Trail every summer and hopes eventually to complete the whole trail. He can still be seen training on our neighborhood sidewalks in all kinds of weather, with a stuffed backpack on his shoulders and walking stick in his grip.

The lessons that Dr. Osborne taught me have made a lasting impression, for sure. I continue to play the flute today whenever I can and still bring my flute to him for occasional tune-ups and repairs. "Flute surgery," I call it. I like knowing that he has been the only person ever to work on my silver flute — the same flute that he recommended that my parents buy for me when I was in eighth grade. I brought it to him at Christmastime for some repairs, and when I picked it up he reminded me that long ago he'd removed more dents from my flute than from that of any other student he has had to this day. "Your flute was the most badly dented instrument I have ever worked on," he reminds me with a laugh. There's nothing like a trip back home every once in a while to keep you humble!

When I think of those who have been mentors to me I also think back to my high school years, when I was lucky enough to find a mentor on the running trails. My high school cross-country coach was a high-energy rail of a man with flaming red hair and a beard to match. He was an absolute running fanatic and a little bit crazy, and I liked him immediately. "Mr. V," as we called him, since his last name was so long, was one of the earliest in a lineup of people whom I now thank for passing on some of life's important lessons.

The first advice he gave me came in the form of tips for buying a good pair of running shoes. He talked about the difference between gel and air cushioning and the advantages and disadvantages of certain brands. At the age of thirteen I got my first pair of running shoes and ran my first two-mile run with Mr. V. He began my training by mapping out some long, slow distance runs (we jokingly referred to this long, slow distance as LSD). Eventually he helped me to build up to the point where I could start some speed work and prepare to race.

Mr. V. taught me that running can be a solitary pursuit, and also that it can be a way to form and nurture relationships with other people. He taught me what it means to run as a member of a team, how you pick up each other's slack when you are running well and another person isn't, how it is vital to cheer for other teammates when you're not racing, and how everyone should wear team shirts to school on race days to show their spirit. "These are just some of the things you do," said Mr. V., "when you are part of a team."

He rejoiced in my triumphs, like qualifying for the state meet and winning medals at big invitational races. He comforted me when I hit a huge performance slump during my junior year after suddenly growing hips and a more adult body. He barked at me when I skipped push-ups during our warm-ups and hugged me when I ran a race in record time. During that killer third mile in a three-mile race he would look right at my pained face as I ran by and say, "Renée, now you're going to have to reach down a little bit." Even though he said this many times, the impact it had on me didn't change. Even now, when I'm confronted with other difficult situations, I think to myself, "Okay Renée, time to reach down a little bit." Little bits of encouragement like this, along with a combination of challenges, affirmations, and personal attention from one outstanding coach, resulted in one of my most formative high school experiences.

I still remember something Mr. V. said to me one of the first times I talked to him. We were in the midst of some of the hottest and most humid August days, and I was nervously anticipating the beginning of high school and an attempt at a new sport. He said to me, "The best thing you can ever do for me is to come see me in twenty years and say, 'Coach, it's been twenty years and I'm still doing it. I still love running.' I'd love it if you would come back some day and tell me that."

At the age of thirteen, twenty years into the future seemed too far away to even consider. Now that time is not far away. I somehow lost track of Mr. V. between my geographical moves and his job changes. I hope I can find him someday. I'd like to tell him about the marathons I've finished, the Saturday morning races I still run with my friends, the anxieties that long runs have soothed, and the ideas these runs have sparked. I'd like to tell him that I still think about his shoe-buying advice and have probably purchased about twenty-five pairs of running shoes since those August days. I'd like to tell him about the difference he made in my life.

Mr. V. and Dr. Osborne helped to cultivate interests that I believe will be lifelong, or at least for as long as my knees and lungs hold out. These two mentors taught me that these pursuits can be solitary and they can also be shared; they can be harnessed for the service of others. Music and running have continued to be integral parts of my vocation. As other interests of mine have waxed and waned, come and gone, these two pursuits have remained constant. I see both as fulfilling me personally and enabling me to serve others. It is running that keeps my heart healthy and my muscles strong and flexible. It is running that has generated many insights and provided a healthy physical and emotional outlet at the end of difficult days. It is music that has filled both my own soul and the souls of others who have listened to me play the flute. It is very gratifying that I can still share my musical talents with people at my church, that I can offer running advice to a friend who is trying to lose weight, and that I can more fully experience the wondrous change in seasons by running year-round. As I reflect on my own vocation, I continue to see running and music as fundamental parts of it. The fact that I have had lasting relationships with generous experts in these pursuits has been invaluable.

Often, during our early years, mentors come in the form of teachers, professors, and coaches. My friend Emily, who is a professional sculptor, has had a similar positive experience with a good mentor. She met her mentor and professor, Gary, during her first college course in sculpture. She recalls talking to this quiet and unassuming teacher after class one day about her uncertainty as to the course of her studies. "I had, I think, five different majors at the time," she said, "but knew that I really liked art. Gary told me that he had noticed that I had potential, that he could tell that I liked it." She had recognized this potential as well, yet she struggled with whether she would be able to make a living with art as a career. Emily thought that perhaps something art-related with some marketability would be the best option, for example, a career in graphic design. She mentioned graphic design to Gary and he said to her immediately, "I *cannot* see you doing that and being happy."

"This was a two-second conversation," she said, "but Gary does not say very much, so I knew he felt strongly that he was right about me not liking graphic design. He told me not to worry about the future so much." This indeed turned out to be very good advice for Emily. When she talks about her career in art, which is now beginning to flourish, she speaks of a series of doors that have opened up to her. "Doors keep opening, one by one, and I keep walking through them, one by one," she says. "I just try to look at the door that is right in front of me."

Emily's later conversations with Gary revealed that his own career as an artist unfolded in a very similar fashion. He taught high school art for a few years, pursued his master's in art, and now teaches at the college level. He is loved and respected by his students. Though Emily is now finished with college, she still communicates with Gary on a regular basis. "What makes Gary such a good mentor is that he is so accessible," she says. "We e-mail each other all the time. He is very dedicated to the people in his life, even students whom he taught for only a quarter. Gary is very committed to keeping up with the relationships he has established."

For Emily, a relationship that began with a striking two-second conversation has developed into her most formative professional relationship to this day. Currently, she is gathering all her current works together for her first art exhibit at a local arts center. A brief yet incisive comment from a mentor, combined with her talent and hard work, has gone a long way.

Though some mentors have made their impact through an enduring and lasting relationship, others exercise their influence through brief interactions or little tidbits of advice they share during short conversations. I can recall a number of pithy aphorisms passed on by important people in my life. "Expenses will always rise to meet income," says my dad. "Be brilliant, be brilliant," said a graduate school professor. "Never let your classes interfere with your education," said an academic adviser. "Never, ever, give up on friendships," said a priest friend.

Mentoring Means "Come on Over"

When I think of those mentors who have made a big impact in a short time, I think back to a graduate student who taught one of my college courses. I remember very little about the content of what he actually taught me, but one memory from outside the classroom stands out in my mind. Bill hosted a group of students for dinner one night after class. He prepared a wonderful dinner for us — pasta, salad, bread, and dessert. The meal was a welcome change from dining hall food, and at the time it was an exciting novelty to be invited to a teacher's house for dinner.

There was something special about the atmosphere in the home that Bill and his wife owned. The living room was bright and colorful with lots of chairs and couches. The decorations were not fancy or elaborate but obviously had been chosen with great care. When I commented on how comfortable the living room was, Bill smiled. "Oh yeah, thanks. My wife used to work at Crate and Barrel so we got a lot of our furniture that way." He spoke of how they had recently gotten married and moved into the house, and how they enjoyed setting it up and finding places for their newly acquired furniture.

At one point in the evening, on my way through the kitchen, I peeked into the open doorway to Bill and his wife's bedroom. The furniture in the bedroom was carefully arranged and comfortable, but much simpler than the living room furniture. I realized that they had probably very intentionally focused on decorating the living room first. The room that guests would occupy was obviously a priority.

Though Bill never said a word about hospitality, at that moment it became very clear to me how important it was to him and his wife. The way they had decorated their home spoke volumes, not to mention that he had gone out of his way to cook dinner for his students. After eating at Bill's house I thought of how important meals were to Jesus and his disciples, and how Jesus practiced hospitality in the way he lived. I also thought of these words attributed to Francis: "Preach the Gospel, and use words if necessary."

At that dinner I learned a lot, even though there was no lecture, no reading preparation, and no test. I made a commitment that night to try to be a person who embodied hospitality, someone who put my guests first. When later I taught that same course as a graduate student I cooked dinner for my students as well, after both semesters. All of them came, despite their crazy college schedules, each remarking how nice it was to be in a "real" home eating "real" food. I enjoyed being on the other end of the experience, and was even more appreciative of Bill for giving me the idea and showing me the importance of hospitality. Though my relationship with him was brief, that one dinner I shared at his home made a lasting impression, so much so that I wanted to do things exactly as he had done. I am reminded of something Henri Nouwen once wrote, that "true ministry duplicates itself."

Hospitality seems to be an important characteristic of a good mentor, though hospitality doesn't necessarily include food. Two married friends of mine, John and Sylvia, view their mentoring relationships with young people as an act of hospitality. They share an office on a college campus and have done so for years. John and Sylvia are in their fifties now and have guided hundreds of young couples through the exciting and arduous process of marriage preparation. "The focus of our work is providing an open space where people can discover themselves," says Sylvia. "We try our best to provide a free and friendly space where young couples can grapple with questions. We aren't going to tell them what to do, but we give suggestions of the kinds of issues they should be talking about. We let the couples do the work. We're just the facilitators, not an advice-giving business! There are often no definitive answers to the questions that come up during the marriage preparation process. Neat and tidy answers are often hard to come by."

Sylvia brings up an important point. We shouldn't believe for a moment that one person has all of the answers. In fact, sometimes the best mentors are not the ones who give us an answer, but give us more questions to consider. The best mentors often answer a question with another question.

John and Sylvia's work entails providing resources for engaged couples — articles, books, and other reading material on the subject of relationships. But the bulk of their mentoring takes place through the sharing of their own insights and experiences, and this includes sharing their own failures. "Sometimes we give a couple advice and after they leave, we turn to each other and say, 'Wow, that is pretty good advice — we should try doing that!'" said Sylvia with a laugh.

Through the sharing of stories about their own marriage, John and Sylvia try to give couples realistic expectations about what they can expect from their marriages. "We don't want to take away the mystery for them," said John. "We just want to prepare them for what they might face, and alleviate their fears about divorce and dysfunction they see in their own families. In discussing what marriage might entail we try to find a balance between idealism and realism."

John and Sylvia affirm that they probably do their best mentoring in their unconscious moments, the in-between times when they don't even feel that they are really working. Just by the very fact that they live and work together, they are witnessing to the strength of their own partnership. John says he enjoys when young adults ask him, "How can you guys work together and be married?" "It just reminds us of why we enjoy working together and being married to each other," he says. "It forces us to keep thinking about that question and to answer it in new ways."

Though it is best to have a mentor who shares our physical surroundings, there certainly is much to learn from mentors whom we are separated from by geography or time. Many times I've learned things as I have observed someone from afar, often without their knowing it. There are some people I would consider as mentors, even though we have never even met. I feel this way about authors of the books I've turned to in the few minutes before I drift off to sleep each night. Many have provided me with final "food for thought" for the day, the "dessert," if you will, at day's end. These authors comprise an eclectic mix of vintage, style, and sophistication: Kathleen Norris, Barbara Kingsolver, Anna Quindlen, F. Scott Fitzgerald, Frank McCourt, and Harper Lee. From each I've learned valuable lessons about writing and about the different ways to live a good life. All these authors, through their reflections, have stretched my mind and enlarged my worldview. Their words have added grist for the mill of my mind and have shaped who I am. I have quoted some of them throughout this book. Though I have never met any of them, I still consider them mentors.

In discerning your vocation having a few good mentors is invaluable. Within your chosen profession or lifestyle it always helps to have your eye on a few people you feel have "done things right." These can be people you admire from a distance or those whom you have exposure to on a day-to-day basis. They can be people with whom you share a profession or simply people whom you admire for the way they live. I hope the stories I have shared have indicated that a variety of good mentors has been a guiding force in my own life. By observing and listening to the advice of "my elders," as I affectionately call them, I can learn from their example and adapt their advice to my own life situation. Though there are some lessons you can learn only by discovering them yourself — otherwise known as "learning things the hard way" — it always helps to have a few consultants along the way.

Our mentors can serve as a conduit for God's communication with us. I firmly believe that God speaks to us and calls us through the voices of our mentors. God works through the hands, voices, and examples of our mentors. A mentor's generosity and willingness to devote time and energy to us is God's generosity pouring forth through another person. God calls forth our gifts through our mentors. The molding and shaping that a good mentor provides is God's molding and shaping. In the words of the prophet Isaiah, "God, we are the clay, and you are the potter; we are all the work of your hand." God works through our mentors to shape us into the person we are called to be.

Our mentors are much more than sources of information — they are living examples and founts of wisdom. They are both givers of advice and living proof that their wisdom can be lived. Their wisdom that comes from life experience is decidedly different from the vast amounts of information that we have at our disposal. Within minutes, given a computer with a fast modem or a good server, I can find dozens of good websites and print out reams of information on any given topic. I can go to a library or dial a toll-free number to get any information I need. Information is good, and it is indeed helpful. But information is no substitute for wisdom.

Wisdom comes packaged as a living, human example, the best possible teacher and mentor. Wisdom is packed with meaning in a way that information isn't. Wisdom has a human face. Wisdom is information with soul. Imagine if, in the movie *The Karate Kid,* Mr. Miyagi had simply handed Daniel a thick manual of martial arts instructions and illustrations instead of taking the time to teach him the beautiful and powerful discipline of karate. Chances are, Daniel would never have learned the profound life lessons Mr. Miyagi taught him through the discipline of karate.

What's Apparent about Parents

In any discussion about vocation or mentors it is good (and often very revealing) to take a look at our own parents' vocational decisions and how their choices have affected ours. Sometimes we underestimate the impact their mentorship has had on us. Many of us are children of those in the Baby Boom generation — those who were born from the mid-1940's to the mid-1960's. Pundits and sociologists often describe the Baby Boomers as a generation obsessed with success and consumed by their work. Supposedly, the next generation, our generation, whether we are called "Gen Xers" or "the MTV generation," is the generation of slackers plagued by leaden indifference to prestigious careers or the hot-button political issues that were so important to our parents. Caricatures of Generation X often include words like "spoiled," "materialistic," and "apathetic." We are sometimes referred to as the generation that would rather purchase four-dollar lattes than save money for our retirement. There is a perceived tension between the Baby Boomers and the Gen Xers because of their different priorities and lifestyle choices.

It is difficult (and quite unfair, I believe) to attempt to classify an entire generation. Sometimes it is helpful, though, to look at generational differences on a case-by-case basis, especially in terms of how our parents' vocational decisions have affected and guided the choices we make now. Whether we like it or not, the ideologies, beliefs, and values that we hold come in large measure from our parents, our first and most influential mentors. Though I sometimes cringe when I hear myself repeating the same things my dad or mom used to say to me — the things I swore I would *never* repeat — I am very grateful for the life lessons they've passed on to me over the years. The lessons I speak of, for the most part, are not ones spoken to me. They were lessons passed on through actions — not one-time only actions, but actions and gestures that were repeated and consistent. Discrete acts added up over time to become habitual for my family, and thus are habitual for me now. This consistency reminds me of something my friend Sara says, that one has to do something twenty-one times before it becomes a habit. Our habits form our character and are an integral part of our vocation. It is often our parents who cultivated some of our first habits, many of which are now ingrained us.

Though I probably couldn't name twenty-one instances right now, I can recall many situations in which my parents cultivated a strong sense of social justice within our family. Instilling a social conscience was just one of the many ways my parents have served as mentors. Their commitment to justice manifested itself as it pertained to individuals, to our community, and to our environment. I think back now to a host of examples that conveyed to me that having a social conscience was very important. I remember bringing baskets of Christmas dinner to needy families, and I recall how my brother was praised for giving his bike away to a boy who had never owned a bike. These gestures were small, yet they conveyed that our family's circle of concern was to extend beyond the bounds of our comfortable neighborhood. What was important was that these gestures were consistent. My parents carried out these good deeds repeatedly and thus created a way of life for our family.

During my childhood and teenage years I learned the importance of being a conscientious consumer. On more than one occasion I duked it out with my mom when she wouldn't let me buy clothes with brand names plastered across the front. "You're placing too much importance on a name," she would say to me. Though my mom occasionally gave in when I pleaded and begged for the Benetton sweatshirt or the Esprit book bag, we had extensive conversations about how brand names were for snobs, or for people who placed more importance on looks than what lay underneath.

As a teenager I thought nothing would be more tragic than not wearing what everyone else was wearing. I fought with my mom tooth and nail about clothes. Now, though I still battle my materialistic impulses regularly, I feel free from at least some of the concern with having the "right" car or wearing the "right" brand of clothes. As a result of the conversations with my mom I don't automatically trash anything with a recognizable brand name, but I feel that those challenging conversations we had during my tumultuous teenage years have given me some valuable critical sensibilities that continue to inform the purchases I make.

While my mom fought the battles with me over clothes, my dad taught me the importance of supporting local businesses when at

all possible. Thursdays were his days off from work, and sometimes we would run errands together after school. My dad loves to
read, and errands with him often involved a trip to a bookstore to
pick up a book he'd read a review of in the newspaper. We would
patronize a small, locally owned bookstore downtown instead of
shopping at the mega-bookstore in the strip mall a few miles away.
"Now, this book is going to cost more here," he would say to me,
"but it is good to support a business that is owned locally." He
practiced the same commitment to local businesses in his choice
of restaurants and hardware stores, and I find myself trying to do
the same thing whenever I can.

It was also my dad who taught me the importance of having
a responsible relationship to the environment. He built a set of
wooden compost bins in our backyard where we could toss our
watermelon rinds, coffee grounds, and apple peels, which in turn,
provided fertilizer for the garden. An unexpected bonus was that
a pumpkin patch sprouted up right next to the compost bin and
continues to provide huge pumpkins and squash every fall. Habit-
ually using the compost bins and the five or six different recycling
containers lining the garage wall when I was young has helped
me to be a more environmentally conscious adult.

My parents' sense of justice extended to the church as well. I remember in high school, on more than one occasion, when priests
would invite my brother to dinner, hoping, presumably, that he
might be interested in the priesthood. My parents were uncomfortable with this and did not encourage him to go to dinner. It was not
the vocation to the priesthood that they disagreed with, but rather
that only one of their children was being invited. I remember my
mom saying to me more than once, "They should be inviting you,
too. I don't like them excluding you from these opportunities."

Though I didn't realize it at the time, my mom's concern with
this issue communicated volumes to me about my own role in the
church. Because of her, I realize that I have a role in the church,
and a valued one at that. Because of her I realize that the church
needs my gifts and talents, and I have a responsibility to share
them with a faith community. In turn, I realize that the church
should value the time and talent that I share. The cultivation of a

social conscience is just one of the many ways my parents have mentored me and influenced my choices.

Friends of mine have shared with me how their parents' roles as mentors have affected their own vocational decisions. One friend in particular comes to mind immediately. She and her husband Kevin have been married for two years, and she is now five months pregnant with their first child. They are starting to make arrangements with their work supervisors and have begun to discuss how they are going to balance both their careers once the baby is born. My friend struggles with her conflicting desires to be present to the baby and yet to maintain an active professional life. "My mom always stayed home with my brother and me, and I really feel like I benefited from that," she said to me. "At the same time, I can't imagine being home all day. I know my mom feels strongly that I should stay home because she loved it and it worked out very well for her. Yet I always want to have at least *some* kind of professional life. I hope my husband and I can work this out." Though she will listen to her mother's advice, my friend will be the one to make her own decision. It is good that she recognizes where her desire to stay home comes from, and is able to balance that with her own opinions and concerns as well as those of her husband.

They're Only Human

Inevitably, it happens. When we first meet or learn about potential mentors we put them on a pedestal. We admire them uncritically, wondering how they learned all that they learned, how they got to be so talented, how they landed such a great lifestyle or career. And then, as our relationship with them deepens, as it becomes more real and authentic, we see their human side, which we weren't privy to before, when our relationship was more distant. We see that their houses are messy, like ours, that they are having marital troubles with their spouse, or that they don't have all of the answers. We realize that they are on the same journey we are, though they may be farther along the road. Sometimes it is easy to become disillusioned when we discover the faults, limits, and quirks of our mentors. We somehow want them to be bigger than life, and we're disappointed when we discover that, of course, they aren't.

I remember feeling a sense of disillusionment after having a one-on-one conversation with one of my college professors. She was brilliant, dynamic, funny, and delivered excellent lectures that left my mind spinning and reeling with possibility as I walked out of class. I decided I wanted to be just like her and grew to admire her a great deal. Early in the semester, after hearing a few of her lectures, I decided that I wanted to meet with her one-on-one. I couldn't wait to have a discussion with her about some of the issues that had been raised in class and thought that I might seek some career advice from her. I checked my syllabus to see when her office hours were and made sure to get to her office right when they began, so I would have as much time with her as possible.

Our late afternoon meeting was anything but what I expected. In person, in the confines of her office, my professor was quite quiet and reserved. Our conversation was awkward, and getting her to talk was like pulling teeth. I suddenly felt very shy, inarticulate, and confused. Where was the dynamic woman I encountered in the huge lecture hall on Tuesdays and Thursdays? Did she not want to talk to me? I left her office after about ten minutes, feeling embarrassed and disappointed and wondering what I had done wrong.

I realize now that my professor was very shy, and while she was an excellent teacher and lecturer, she wasn't as comfortable in one-on-one meetings as she was in the classroom. There is a sort of comforting distance that one feels in large groups that often vanishes when the group size shrinks, and she obviously felt more comfortable in the former setting.

Our awkward ten-minute meeting taught me an important lesson: we can't expect our mentors to be the end-all-be-all. Their gifts and limitations balance each other out, just like ours do. We know this intellectually, but it still can be disappointing when we experience this reality for the first time. Our mentors are human, just like we are. Learning this and experiencing this makes our relationship with them all the more real, all the more authentic.

I hope that someday when I serve as mentor to others that my future mentees will give me lots of latitude when they discover that I'm human too. I hope they'll be willing to look the other way when they come over for dinner and see that my kitchen is a mess. I hope they aren't disappointed when they see the file folder full of rejection letters by my desk. I hope they treat me with compassion when they learn that I don't have all the answers to life's difficult questions. And yet I hope they remember me as someone who doesn't try to hide her limits and shortcomings.

Maybe my mentees will realize, as I have, that we can learn just as much from the manner in which our mentors deal with their shortcomings as we can from the way they share their gifts. As we listen for the voice of vocation through our mentors, we gradually realize that gifts and limitations come hand-in-hand. Sometimes it is in learning that our mentors are fully human, just like we are, that the greatest learning begins.

❧ Eight ❧

Road Rules

From everyone who has been given much, much will be required; and to whom they entrusted much, of them they will ask all the more.
　　　　　　　　　　　　　　　　　　　　—Luke 12:48

Running marathons is wonderful. I absolutely love it. Lots of other people do too, especially people who are in our age group. For the past few years over thirty thousand people have run the Chicago Marathon, a good number of them in their twenties and thirties. There is something about long-distance running that seems to be contagious for members of our generation.

There are few things better than standing on the start line of a race, wrapped in the coolness of morning, surrounded by thousands of other people who are just as crazy as you are, in anticipation of the big 26.2-mile journey. I enjoy the pre-race chatter as we jog in place both to stave off nervousness and keep warm. There is excitement in the air, to be sure.

For many people, unless they happen to be one of the world champion runners from Kenya or Morocco, the marathon itself lasts for three or four hours. This is a long time to run continuously!

As the starting horn blares and I hear the "beep" of the electronic race chip attached to my shoe, I begin to shuffle my feet with a mixture of dread and anticipation, weaving my way through the enormous crowd. I'm not sure how my legs and lungs will hold up, but I know that I will have many people to run with along the way. Crowds of people lining the racecourse will encourage me when I am fatigued. There will be aid stops with water and sport drinks at every mile marker, places to refuel and get my energy level back up.

At some points along the marathon course I will feel like I am on top of the world. I know from experience that I will probably cruise through the first thirteen miles without a problem. Adrenaline will surge through my veins, I will smile and wave at the crowds. I may even skip some of the water stops.

But then, after mile 13, almost imperceptibly, gradually, things will begin to change, mile by mile. By mile 18 my spirits will be drooping, my legs will start to ache, and I will begin to doubt my abilities. By mile 24, my running buddies and I will have split up after staying together for miles, due to the variation in our stamina and muscle strength. I will face the rest of the race among strangers. I'll try to give myself mental pep talks, inner encouragement.

Finally, at mile 25, when I realize that I am on the home stretch, my spirits and running pace will pick up. I will know that I *can* finish, that I do have it within me to complete that last mile. I will cross the finish line with a mixture of exhaustion and elation but mostly a sense of triumph. My thoughts will be mixed: "I am *never* doing that again," and "I would *love* to do that again."

A marathon in a way mirrors many of young adulthood's ups and downs. On the journey through our twenties, we cannot do it alone. We need the support of "fellow runners" and those who volunteer at the water and refreshment stands, people who help us keep our energy up. We wish we could always feel like we do during the first thirteen miles of the marathon, full of anticipation and energy, confidence and potential. But often our energy will be drained and our faith will be tested. Our muscles and our spirits will be tired. We may feel as if we are traveling life's journey among strangers. When we make it through a difficult period, however, when we struggle across the finish line once more, we will feel drained but also more confident in our ability to live through the trials that life presents us. We face each new journey a little bit wiser, having learned how to endure and having picked up a few training tips that will keep us in good shape for whatever life asks of us. Ultimately we develop both the discipline and endurance to keep going through whatever lies ahead. I'm reminded of a tiny framed saying on my bedroom wall: "The race is not always to the swift . . . but to those who keep on running." In the discernment and discovery of our vocation, the journey will be full of both "mile 13" experiences and "mile 25 experiences." There will be days when we need lots of water and refreshment. And there will be days when we feel so in love with our vocational path, so confident, that we feel like we could run forever.

Another type of journey that our generation, like our Baby Boomer parents, seems to have perfected, is the planning of a good road trip. There are few things that are more fun than the anticipation of a weekend road trip, whether it takes us to a friend's wedding, Elvis's birthplace, the beach, or a backpacking adventure in the mountains. Like at the beginning of a race, at the onset of a weekend road trip there is a sense of excitement and anticipation.

During the year that I lived in Seattle, my friends and I perfected the art of the road trip, especially during those times when we planned our weekend hikes all over western Washington. We spent the few days before each trip looking at guidebooks and maps, plotting the duration of our hike, and estimating the driving distance to the trailhead. We checked the weather the night before and tried to anticipate snow, mud, fallen trees, or any other adverse conditions. The night before our departure we packed sandwiches, fruit, and trail mix in our backpacks. We scanned our maps and filled up our cars with gas.

Those Saturday road trips to Olympic National Park, the western Cascades, and the San Juan Islands provide some of my best memories from my time in Seattle. Sometime the trip would go exactly as we had planned, and other times we would find other trails to explore. Sometimes we had to change our course due to the poor condition of a trail. Many times we were surprised by a gorgeous vista or a shimmery alpine lake that we hadn't planned on seeing. Occasionally, weather would force us to spend our afternoon in a diner near the trailhead.

Regardless of what happened on our weekend hikes in Seattle, I came to understand during that year that there is something very special about the planning, experiencing, and reflecting back on a journey. In the discovery of our vocation, along the way it is good to follow a practice similar to that of the road trip: plan, experience, and reflect back on the experience. Be prepared for surprises, both the pleasant and the unpleasant, both the shimmery alpine lakes and the bad weather. After each journey, ask yourself, "What is one thing that I will take with me from this experience?" If we are reflective about our "mini-journeys," our weekend road trips, our brief encounters with life's adventures, we will encounter each new "mini-journey" enriched and with heightened awareness.

Journeys, whether they take the form of marathons, road trips, service opportunities, or spiritual travels, are the stuff of life. The discernment of our vocation is a lifelong journey that will encompass significant relationships, setbacks, opportunities, gifts, moments of clarity, and moments of uncertainty. The journey is lifelong. One of the biggest misconceptions about vocation is that the discovery of one's vocation is a momentary happening, an instant epiphany, or a lightning bolt that illuminates the rest of our life's path. The discovery of our vocation is, rather, a process, a journey. There may be significant, discrete moments of clarity along the way, but there is always more to be discovered and discerned. On the vocational journey we never "arrive." We are always "arriving." The vocational road trip lasts much longer than a significant weekend.

Discerning our vocation is a process of continuing conversion, of continually opening ourselves up to our deepest, most heart-felt desire, which is, ultimately, God's desire for us. There will be times along the way when we can rest, times when we are satisfied with our friends, our prayer life, our career, our place in the world. There will be just as many occasions, however, that we will feel that things are "not quite right," that maybe we are not dating the right person or that maybe there is a career out there that is better for us. This restlessness, a vital part of a journey, is just as important to take note of as the times in which we are at peace. We must pay attention to our restlessness, for it is our restlessness, our penchant for the journey, that will drive us to God. Unrest is good for us in that it keeps us moving forward on our vocational journey. In the words of St. Augustine, "Our hearts are restless until we rest in you." Contemporary author Ronald Rolheiser, in his book *The Holy Longing,* describes this restlessness as desire:

> Whatever the expression, everyone is ultimately talking about the same thing — an unquenchable fire, a restlessness, a longing, a disquiet, a hunger, a loneliness, a gnawing nostalgia, a wildness that cannot be tamed, a congenital all-embracing ache that lies at the center of human experience and is the ultimate force that drives everything else. This dis-ease is universal. Desire gives no exemptions.

Whether we call it restlessness, desire, or dis-ease, we all have a type of unrest that has the potential to drive us to God. Our vocation is about what we do with that unrest, that desire, that dis-ease. We will be restless until we are living most fully the life that God calls us to live, and this will take a lifetime. Vocation is about providing a channel, a direction, a funnel for our restlessness.

In this final chapter I've reflected a bit on the image of the journey, using the specific metaphors of the marathon and the road trip, and how journey relates to the theme of vocation. Now, by way of closure and conclusion, I'd like to share a few other tips and tools that people have recommended to me along the way. In this great road trip we call life it helps to have a few "road rules" to live by, disciplines and tools to strengthen us and nourish us for the journey.

Welcome Other Generations

In many of the jobs that I have held thus far, I have been blessed to form close relationships with co-workers who are, shall we say, quite a few years older than me. I affectionately call them "my elders." We constantly joke about our generational differences and the different cultural settings we have grown up in. For example, we don't share preferences for actors or actresses, singers or songwriters. This difference manifested itself in an office conversation with my boss. "I can't *believe* you've never heard of Rosemary Clooney," he said to me incredulously one day at lunch. "How could you have never heard any of her music? What year were you born?" He continued to shake his head in disbelief. Despite my listing of all the facts I knew about her nephew, George Clooney, despite my claims to have watched countless of *ER* episodes that he starred in, my boss continued to shake his head.

And, of course, he had never heard of any of the names printed on the CD cases I stack by my desk so I can listen to music on my computer throughout the day. He looks at my camping thermos that I bring to lunch as if it were a small pipe bomb. "We have glasses here you can drink out of," he reminds me. My co-workers and I tease each other about our different tastes in food — their preference of meat and potatoes versus my preference for spicy burritos, giant bagels, and fruits and vegetables. We only need to sit down at the lunch table to realize that, because of the simple fact that we are members of different generations, we are very, very different.

It is tempting to spend all our time with people our own age, but those in other generations, particularly older generations, have much in the way of life experience to share with us. There are some life lessons one can learn only by living, and not from a book. I think of one morning in particular when I was struck by the older generations' collective wisdom in a profound way. I was attending Mass at my parish, and the priest announced that it was the feast of Isaac Jogues, a Jesuit saint. The Gospel reading from Luke asserted that God knows us so well that even the hairs of our heads are all counted.

In the homily, before delving into the scriptures of the day, the presider supplied us with some interesting data: "They say the heads of blonds contain 150,000 hairs; brunettes, about 125,000; and redheads, 100,000 hairs," he said. As I looked all around me that morning I saw very few blonds, brunettes, or redheads. Instead, I observed a sea of white, gray, and salt-and-pepper hair.

As if reading my mind, the presider said, "I'm not sure about white." A white-haired woman (sitting next to her balding husband) piped in, "Definitely less!" and we all laughed. I smoothed my dark brown hair self-consciously, suddenly with a sharpened realization that in twenty years, maybe thirty if I am lucky, my hair would be gray as well.

During a closing announcement the congregation learned that in our midst was a couple celebrating their forty-fourth wedding anniversary. I had been watching the two of them that morning, marveling at how long they have been married and how well they must know each other, how many meals they have shared, how many sacrifices they have made. They appeared to be so content and fulfilled. I looked upon them as people who had "made it," faithful to each other for forty-four years. I wanted to approach them after Mass and ask, "So what is your secret?"

At Mass that day I started to realize that "my elders," the people I celebrated that liturgy with, know a few things that our generation does not. They are just more experienced, period. They've gone to school and made their livings, raised their children and now enjoy their grandchildren. They've endured years of marital trials, national tragedies, and family celebrations. Some have celebrated more than seventy Christmases. Over a lifetime they've discovered that spending time with a faith community enriches their lives, and they understand this truth better than our generation does now.

Older generations are characterized by a loyalty that our culture-of-choice generation is not. I am a "church-shopper" myself. At times I have attended certain parishes with regularity, but just as often I have switched from parish to parish, each time hoping to find something "better," something more inspiring. Yet there is something in the older generation's loyalty that I find attractive. Their loyalty gives them authority, ownership of their community.

Older generations are in touch with truths that our generation is not yet capable of grasping. Writer Kathleen Norris observes this same phenomenon when she describes her own faith community in her autobiography *The Virgin of Bennington:* "I was drawn to the strong old women in the congregation. Their well-worn Bibles said to me, 'There is more here than you know.' "

As I sat in church that day, a neophyte among the wise, I was overwhelmed by that sense that there was much, much more there than I knew. I could see it in the way they came back to the same place, week after week. They knew something about how the gift of faith can enrich a single life, a family routine. That is one reason I keep coming back. I hope someday to know more of what they know.

Make Time for Silence

"Silence is full of what we need to learn about ourselves," says Joan Chittister. It is often in the silence that God speaks to us, rather than in the buzz of activity that fills most of our days. It is in the silence that our hearts are finally quiet enough to listen for God's voice. To make time for silence is an important practice in the discernment of a vocation.

Finding opportunities for silence can be a challenge. I know that as soon as I get home from work, the first thing I do after I look at my mail is turn on my stereo. God forbid that I would get my dinner ready without musical accompaniment! And often, when treated to the gift of a quiet Sunday afternoon, my first instinct is to call up a couple of friends. My roommate even needs "background noise" while she sleeps. Every night, even in the winter, she turns on a window fan in her room. Even in department stores, gentle Muzak is piped into the background. There is a part of our human nature that is resistant to silence.

One year during Lent I decided that, instead of giving up chocolate or sweets, as I usually did, I was instead going to give up listening to music and National Public Radio in the car. This proved to be a challenge not only on the ten-minute drive to work but especially on longer weekend trips. (Okay, I admit it, on those trips I did cheat a couple of times and turn on the radio. Five hours of silence was just too much!)

At first, surprisingly, the silence was almost jarring, not having the background buzz of news commentary or music. But during those forty-some days of "car silence" I felt my mind relax after I had been driving for a few minutes. The lack of audio stimulation was freeing. I began to notice the scenery on the way to work in a new way. I noticed the houses in my neighborhood, the people who walked at the same time every morning, the gradual greening of the trees. Allowing the sense of hearing to rest freed up some of my other senses.

I can't say that anything particularly profound happened during that experience of Lent except that I did feel more balanced, more at ease, and more attentive. I felt somehow that during the "car silence" I had been more reflective and prayerful, even though I did not explicitly use that time in the car to pray. I felt that the simple elimination of radio noise had uncluttered my mind and my spirit, just a little bit.

The silence rounded out some of my "sharp edges," caused by my morning nervousness about a work meeting or from my anger on the drive home after a difficult conversation with a colleague. The effect the silence had on me reminded me of the way lake and ocean water smooth the edges of a piece of broken glass, rounding it, buffing it, and muting its color. The seawater and the sand round the sharp edges gently over a long period of time, but the effect is lasting and beautiful, so beautiful that many people collect pieces of beach glass and bring them home to display in a glass jar or dish. Silence works on our hearts and souls the same way water works on beach glass. If we are faithful to the practice of keeping silence on a regular basis over a long period, it gently washes over our edges, smoothing them and making something beautiful in the process. It rounds our sharp edges. Silence unclutters our minds, allowing us to pay attention to new details, freeing up mental space for new insights and reflections. Silence makes our souls beautiful over time.

Have Good Conversations

"Ultimately," said Oscar Wilde, "the bond of all companionship, whether in marriage or in friendship, is conversation." In the discovery of a vocation, finding people that we can have regular, meaningful, honest conversations with is of utmost importance. I am not talking about the conversations in which you plan where you are meeting for drinks after work, or you discuss the merits of the teams you've placed in brackets for your office NCAA pool. Those conversations are good and enjoyable, but if that is the level on which all of our conversations take place, we are missing out.

It is important to find a few people with whom we can address "the big questions" in conversation. These should be people who are serious thinkers, have some depth, and strive to make decisions based on good principles. They can be trained in spiritual direction or close friends. They can be our mentors or they can be our peers.

I have one friend who is known for the thought-provoking questions she asks. A future psychiatrist, she questions stances and assumptions that I have taken for granted and is always able to stir up my conscience when I have settled into complacency. With our busy schedules we rarely have time for extensive conversations, yet we make it a priority to get together at least twice a year. When we do, we don't waste time with small talk. "Okay, LaReau," she says, "tell me what's *really* going on with you." Small talk is unacceptable to her when we get together for in-person visits. Instead, we challenge each other in matters of career, faith, social values, and relationships. An inveterate reader, she tells me about the books she has been reading. I always end these visits with my friend with much to think about. I am grateful to have a friend who does not allow conversation to float at the surface level. Having such meaningful conversations is one of the ways we can grow in our sense of vocation.

It is important to keep our conversations with God at the center of our lives. A regular prayer life and regular conversations with God are vital for the discernment of a vocation. It is good to try all kinds of prayer: rote prayers, reading the Sunday Scripture passages, sitting in silence, singing, writing in a journal, listening to quiet music, participating in the sacraments. All these means of prayer are ways of conversing with God. Throughout our lives the way we converse with God will change, just as our friendships grow and change. What worked for us and made us happy in grade school will certainly not be enough to sustain us now. What sustains us now may not do so in five years. What matters is not so much how we pray but simply that we *do,* and do so regularly and intentionally.

Practice Hospitality

It seems that we have relegated one of life's most sacred and special activities, the sharing of meals, to the car. I am just as guilty as anyone. I cannot count how many times I've brushed bagel crumbs and sesame seeds from the seats of my car. I cannot number the times I have wiped up coffee spills from the dashboard, most of which occurred while I was simultaneously talking on my cell phone, drinking coffee, and trying to navigate a quick lane change. I know I am not alone in these practices, and our habits of eating in the car are just one of the many indications that our culture is sacrificing hospitality for the sake of expediency.

I think it is especially easy to neglect the practice of hospitality when we are in our twenties. Our job demands many long hours of us and we are particularly focused on our careers. The long line of cars in the drive-thrus at Wendy's, McDonald's, and Burger King speaks volumes.

Eric Schlosser, in his *New York Times* bestseller *Fast Food Nation,* criticizes fast food not only for its lack of nutritional value, but also for the values it promotes. Faster is better, and drive-thrus are always available. The value of sitting down to a meal with one's friends or family seems to be quickly diminishing. "We just don't have time to eat together," we say, or "Our schedules are just too different."

Hospitality is not just the stuff of the charming photos in a Martha Stewart magazine. Hospitality is a theological concept. There are many stories in Scripture in which Jesus teaches an important lesson or demonstrates an important practice in the context of a meal. In the Easter story of the Road to Emmaus, it is in the breaking of the bread, the sharing of a meal, that Jesus' disciples first recognize him as the risen Christ. In the telling of parables, Jesus uses images of a banquet to reveal what the Kingdom of God will be like. He promoted radical inclusivity by sharing meals with prostitutes, tax collectors, and other social outcasts. Jesus knew that the company in which one eats makes a powerful statement.

The last time Jesus' disciples were gathered as a group was for a supper, the sharing of a meal. A priest friend pointed out to me that that meal was probably the *worst* meal Jesus and his disciples ever shared, and yet it was probably the *best* they ever shared. It was the worst in that they all were anticipating the pain, suffering, and death of a beloved spiritual leader, and the best in that some very intimate words were spoken between companions in acknowledgment of the closeness of their relationships and the mission that the disciples were to carry out "in memory of me." Mealtimes are often the occasion to reveal our deepest concerns, and that is why hospitality is so important. Think of the many significant discussions you have had with friends or family at the dinner table. Many of us can easily and recall some of the best and the worst. Maybe they were at the same meal!

One night, over dinner at an Italian restaurant, I asked my closest friend to be the maid-of-honor in my wedding. She lives a little over an hour away from where I live, and I drove to her house just so we could go out to dinner together. I had been very tempted to ask her over the phone since we talk pretty frequently, but I resisted. I had a sense that it would be better to ask in person. It was hard to contain myself and to wait, but I did.

I was very glad I waited. I was able to ask her in person and watch the expression on her face. We were able to toast to our friendship with glasses of wine. We shared a leisurely dinner engrossed in conversation about our dating relationships, our friendships, our careers, and our lives. We were enjoying each other's company so much that we didn't even notice that two hours had passed and it had grown dark outside. My friend told me that night that she thought it was the best visit we had ever had. I agreed and shuddered to think that I had almost asked her over the phone to be in my wedding.

I recall the words of a Chicago priest I once knew: "Eating is not just a function. It is an opportunity for a relationship. So don't turn down a chance to share a meal with someone simply because you're not hungry — that would be missing the point!" There is much more to a meal than the food itself.

So even if your apartment is small, have a couple of friends over for dinner. It doesn't matter if the table is a coffee table and your guests are squeezed together on your futon, or if all you serve is chicken fingers and cheese sticks, or if you didn't have quite enough time to clean up your house. What matters is not *how* we practice hospitality, but that we *do* practice hospitality, that we invite people to the table.

In the practice of hospitality we invite others into our lives, take the time for good conversation, and share our stories of success and failure, our worries and our problems that have been resolved. Community is built, and the gift of good conversation is shared.

Spend Time with the Poor

"If you have never in your life spent time with the poor," my college professor challenged me while I was trying to choose an internship, "definitely choose a placement that will give you direct contact with the poor. The experience will be invaluable, and you will learn so much." I took her advice, choosing an internship at a homeless shelter, and found her words to be right on target almost from the beginning.

One of my first assignments at the shelter was to organize the weekly bingo game. I have never been a huge fan of bingo, so I debated its relevance for quite a few weeks. What was I doing organizing a bingo game for homeless people? Shouldn't I be helping them write resumes so they could find jobs? Shouldn't I be serving breakfast in the kitchen? Shouldn't I be leading a Bible study to contribute to their spiritual well-being? Shouldn't I be doing something more productive and useful with them?

My friend Mike and I organized the game each week, sorting through donations for T-shirts, sweatshirts, hats, lotion, and perfume, all of which were popular bingo prizes. Week after week we played bingo in the shelter's kitchen. We must have looked like we were having fun, because each week we had more people than the week before. The crowds grew and grew. I thought to myself, "Well, at least we are providing them with an opportunity to have a little fun. Maybe that in itself is good for them."

But then the following week a poignant statement from one of our bingo players reminded me of another reason I was there. A young man named Sean called out "Bingo!" and we invited him forward to pick out a prize. His response surprised me: "I don't want to pick out a prize. I just want to win at something." Simply to savor the experience of winning was enough for him. His simple response reminded me that we all like to win at something, and these folks were no exception. Most of them, unfortunately, came from a population that had suffered far more losses than wins. They never took winning for granted, because they didn't "win" in life very often.

I left the bingo game that night realizing that I had a responsibility to help provide my friends at the shelter with more opportunities to win, to come out ahead, since many of them had been born behind. I also realized that, though I did not feel like I was doing much, I was indeed providing a service for people by giving them an opportunity to enjoy themselves for a change — and to win, at least in a little way.

I realized that in order to follow the example of Christ I have to seek out the company of the poor as he did. This is a challenge that will be with me for the rest of my life, and right now I know that I am not doing enough. Yet spending time with the poor is just as much a spiritual discipline as is attending Mass or making time for personal prayer.

The poor are the face of Christ to us. Often they are the ones to show us what is truly important in life: to feed and to be fed, to nurture and be nurtured, to have and give opportunity, to love and to be loved, to have faith and to share faith.

In working with the both the homeless and the working poor, I have been honored by their openness and honesty. I have been amazed by how readily they share their personal struggles. They are so different from the majority of people I spend my day with in a suburban, educated environment. Most people I encounter there are so guarded and private, so seemingly put together. Yet in the poor there is an openness that I find so inspiring, heartening, and refreshing. They do not pretend to have it all together.

At one time I thought, incorrectly, that those in low-income situations would have no energy left for prayer or spirituality because they would be so spent and drained from trying to acquire their basic material needs. I have found the exact opposite to be true. Many of my poor friends have a very close relationship with God.

They are people of deep faith who value both their personal relationship with Jesus and their connection with the institutional church. Many speak of the support they find in their faith communities. Many spend entire Sundays worshiping and socializing with their faith communities.

The poor are the face of Christ to us; we, in turn, can be the face of Christ to the poor. In the famous words of St. Teresa of Avila:

Christ has no body now on earth but yours.
Yours are the hands with which Christ can bless the world.
Yours are the eyes with which Christ can shine compassion
        on a troubled world.
Yours are the feet with which Christ walks to do good.
Christ has no body but yours,
no hands,
no feet,
no eyes on earth
but yours.

It is not just the materially poor I have in mind. I am also thinking of those who are referred to in the Scriptures as "poor in spirit," those who battle depression, addiction, family difficulties, or a physical or mental handicap. The poor in spirit are often in circumstances just as dire as those without food, drink, shelter, or employment.

My grandfather, though not materially poor, has endured his own battle with a debilitating handicap that threatened to destroy his spirit. For over twelve years he has lived with the use of only one leg after an amputation necessitated by complications from cancer. At the time he underwent the operation my family did not know how he would cope with this devastating loss. We knew that the aftermath of such a major operation required monumental physical adjustments: driving with a different leg, using crutches every day, adapting to more limited mobility, enduring the "phantom pain" that often accompanies the loss of a limb.

My grandfather's coping skills were commendable. He continued to drive regularly, taking yearly trips to Florida with my grandmother. He maintained his small jewelry business until he was in his mid-eighties and was always generous with his jewelry. He always had something in hand for the women in our family, although his taste tended to be flashier than ours. He would present a bracelet or ring and say, "These are really popular in the stores with the women now," or, "I thought of you immediately when I saw this." It was so funny that grandpa, in his seventies, was more caught up on the current jewelry trends than we were!

Though I know that there were many days when my grandfather was depressed and despondent in his recuperation from his amputation, he still was somehow able to press on in his recovery with a spirit of optimism. I remember talking to my grandmother on the phone, months after my grandfather's operation, and hearing him whistle in the background, a sound I had associated with him since childhood. I felt that as long as he was whistling he was doing okay.

I learned many lessons from my grandfather about living life to the fullest, even in the face of adversity and great physical obstacles. But perhaps the most inspiring example was when he came to visit me during my first year of college. My grandmother had died a few years earlier, so he drove by himself. We made plans to go to brunch together, and he said he would pick me up at my dorm in the morning.

The dorm I lived in at the time was a beautiful, Gothic-style building built in the 1920s. Because of the age of the building, there was no elevator for my grandfather to use, and unfortunately I lived on the top floor. Four flights of narrow, steep, well-worn terrazzo stairs led up to our floor, so I knew my grandfather would not be able to see my dorm room. I was disappointed but knew that the stairs would be too much for him at his age on his crutches. I waited in my room, assuming he would call me on the first-floor lobby phone when he arrived.

The phone never rang. Eventually, however, I heard a knock on my door, and there he was, eighty years old, leaning on his crutches, dapperly decked out in a suit, right in front of my room. His forehead was shiny with perspiration, and he had a big smile on his face. "Grandpa, what are you *doing* all the way up here?" I asked, incredulously.

"Did you really think I would come all the way to visit my grand-daughter and not see the room where she lives?" he said with a huge grin. I shook my head and laughed, grateful I had not known that he was climbing those narrow stairs. Live life to the fullest even in the face of adversity. That is the most important lesson I have learned from my grandfather during these years.

I have tried to describe some of the practices I've found to be helpful in building my own life thus far. These practices are not new — I've simply described how they appear through the lens of my own experience. They are tried-and-true practices that have been passed on to me by those who are farther along on life's jour-ney. These practices have been lived and refined by generations of wise and faith-filled people. I hope I have adequately conveyed how valuable these practices are: finding and maintaining rela-tionships with good mentors, becoming a participating member of a faith community, establishing an active and regular prayer life, pursuing meaningful work, serving the poor, and trusting in the hope of the resurrection and all of its ramifications for our lives. If we engage in these practices regularly, or at least strive to do so, they will help us to plumb the depths of our vocation, our call from God.

Epilogue

A Glance Forward

As I write these final words, the late summer is slowly merging with the beginnings of fall. The high school football practices, the rumble of the schoolbuses, and shorter lines at ice cream counters — along with a date circled in heavy black marker on my calendar — remind me that it is time to finish this book. The change in seasons brings with it the usual changes in my work schedule, my weekend pursuits, and the level of activity in my life. I am used to these changes now and make the necessary adjustments: work more hours during the week, travel to football games on some weekends, and carve out more time for writing projects. I now know how this seasonal cycle works in terms of balancing my professional and personal life.

But there is another change this year as I make the transition from summer to fall. As of a few weeks ago, I am now engaged. Had you asked me a year ago if I thought this would happen, I never would have imagined that I would fall in love with an old friend, someone who had already been in my life for ten years. Never would I have guessed that one nervous, frank conversation between friends — in an Irish pub — would change two people's lives so much. "Life is what happens when you are making other plans," as John Lennon put it.

Now I look forward not only to my wedding day but also to blending my life with the life of another person. My fiancé, Jim, and I have been discussing big questions as we make our plans. Just the other day we talked about how we will handle money (or at least how we think we will handle money!). We covered all the practical matters: whether or not to have separate checking accounts and credit cards, who will pay which bills, and how we will budget our incomes and expenses. We talked about how much of our salaries we will give our church and how much we will donate to charities that we believe in. We are aware, through friends who have been there and articles we've read, that differences in the handling of money are a primary source of tension in many marriages.

We've conversed about how much time we will spend with each other's families and how we will balance the careers that are equally important to both of us. I've shared with Jim my decision to keep my last name after we are married. As we discuss all of these important issues I am very mindful of the seriousness and the permanence of it all. I am also conscious that there will be issues and situations we will encounter together that no amount of thoughtful discussion of "what-ifs" will prepare us for. That is a little unnerving, but I find comfort in my sense of certainty that I have chosen the right person to spend my life with.

In the few short weeks that have elapsed since Jim and I made this decision, I have given some thought to what all this means in terms of my vocation. My vocations are many — wife, Catholic, writer, daughter, sister, friend, musician — and to learn how to balance them will take a lifetime. I picture these vocations fitting together like concentric circles, each one building on the one inside that is closer to the core, that small, strong, solid center of the circle that is God. I have to remember the calling that is at the center of those concentric circles, the calling to keep my heart open to God and to the needs of the world.

When Jim proposed to me on the shores of Lake Michigan, he spoke of the need for us both to live with our eyes on God and our feet on the ground. Eyes on God, feet on the ground. Easy to remember, yet no small challenge to live.

Though one vocational question has been answered for me, the question of whether I will be married, I have been surprised at how one answer opens up many new questions. I have grown even more appreciative of the truth that "we never arrive; we are always arriving." We are always traveling, journeying, moving closer to our true vocation. Thank you for sharing this journey with me. May all your travels, spiritual and otherwise, be blessed.

Of Related Interest

Winging It
Meditations of a Young Adult
Therese Johnson Borchard

Honest enriching reflections for men and women in their twenties and thirties on career, friendship, spirituality, suffering, personal growth and much more.

ISBN 1-57075-357-1

God Moments
Why Faith Really Matters to a New Generation
Jeremy Langford

"Jeremy Langford's account of his struggle to find a spiritual home will inspire others to seek God's graceful moments in their own lives."

—Tom Beaudoin, author, *Virtual Faith*

ISBN 1-57075-390-3

Why Not Be a Missioner?
Young Maryknollers Tell Their Stories
Michael Leach and Susan Perry, Editors

Inspiring first-person accounts of young men and women in their twenties and thirties who are serving God and neighbor in every corner of the earth.

ISBN 1-57075-391-1

Please support your local bookstore, or call 1-800-258-5838.

For a free catalogue, please write us at

Orbis Books, Box 308

Maryknoll NY 10545-0308

Or visit our website and order online at
www.orbisbooks.com

Thank you for reading *Getting a Life*. We hope you enjoyed it.